TRACY PORTER'S

HOME STYLE

Follow your *heart* today. *Life* will fall into place once you *make* this a *priority*.

OTHER BOOKS BY TRACY PORTER

Tracy Porter's Dreams from Home

Tracy Porter's Inspired Gatherings

GIFT BOOKS BY TRACY PORTER

Woven in Sunlight—A Garden Companion

Returning Home—The Poetics of Whim and Fancy

Dream with Your Eyes Open

Gentle Influences—The Spirited Ties of Sisters

The Journey Within—A Book of Hope and Renewal

Celebrating Babies

True Love

Walk *down* a path *you have never* traveled . . . *You might just* find *what you are* looking for.

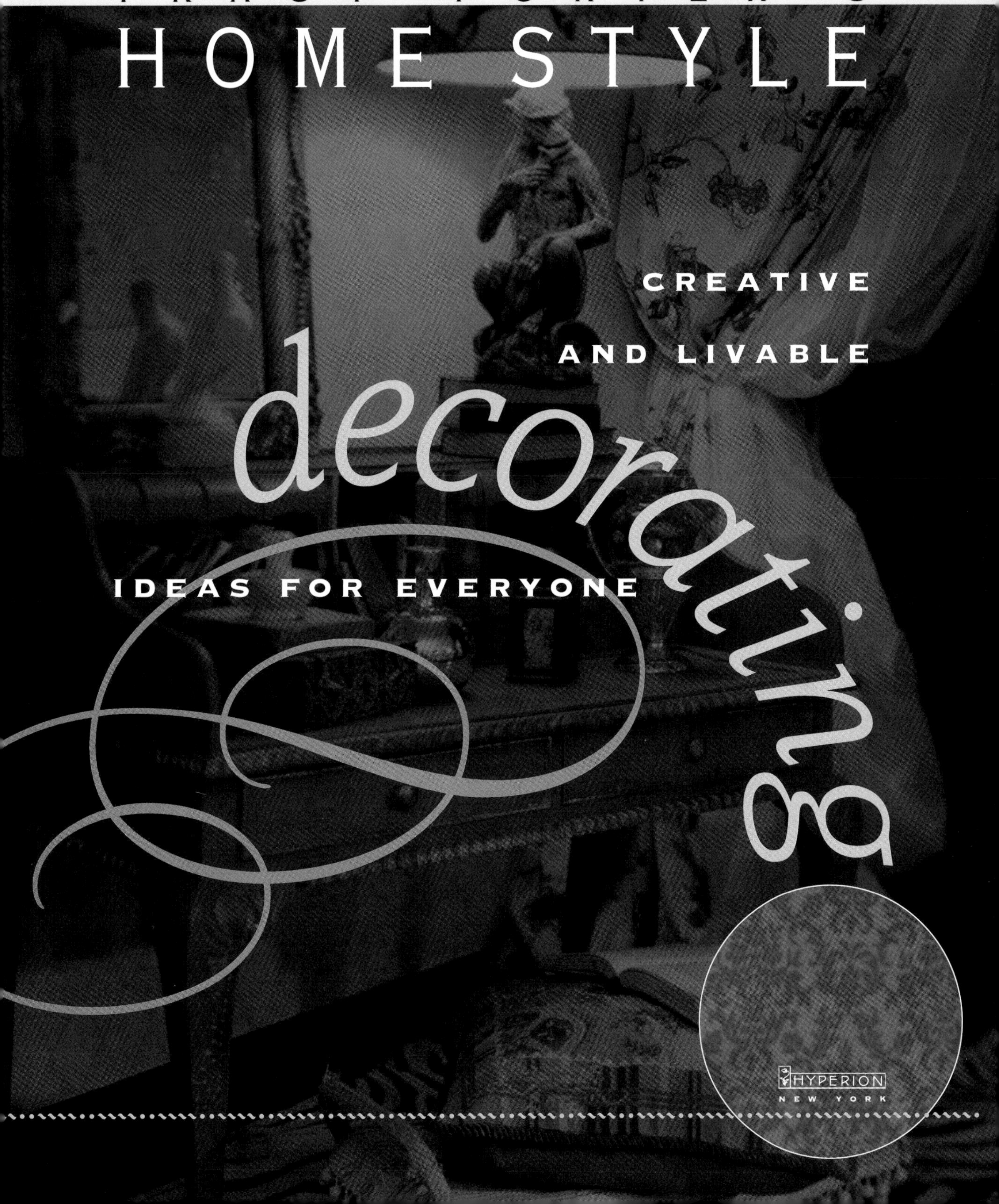

TRACY PORTER'S

HOME STYLE

decorating

CREATIVE

AND LIVABLE

IDEAS FOR EVERYONE

HYPERION
NEW YORK

Copyright © 2002 Tracy Porter

Photography by Katy Rowe and Dale Stenten, Maura Koutoujian, Deborah Fletcher, and Jim Hedrich.

LIBRARY OF CONGRESS CATALOGING-IN-PUBLICATION DATA
Porter, Tracy.
  Tracy Porter's home style: creative and livable decorating ideas for everyone.—1st ed.
    p. cm.
  ISBN 0-7868-6811-2
    1. Handicraft. 2. House furnishings. 3. Interior decoration—Amateurs' manuals. I.
  Title: Home style. II. Title.

  TT157 .P726 2002
  747—dc21   2001039847

                                              Book design by Richard Oriolo

FIRST EDITION

10 9 8 7 6 5 4 3 2 1

FOR MY SWEET CHILDREN—

You make our house a home.

XOXO

ACKNOWLEDGMENTS

THANK YOU TO EVERY DEAR HEART WHO

HAS HELPED IN THE CREATION OF THIS BOOK.

ALL OF YOUR EFFORTS ARE GREATLY

APPRECIATED.

XOXO, T.

CONTENTS

surround

YOURSELF WITH

loveliness!

Our first decorating book! What an exciting project this has been to wrap our arms around. In a fantasy world, it would have been great to stop time and devote ourselves solely to this creation. But we, like most of you, are in the midst of a balancing act every single day. Our priorities as individuals and as a company are constantly being refined. I have many things going on in my personal life that are helping to mold my perspective. I've had a wonderful and fulfilling year, as our twin boys, Max & Fin, will be celebrating their second birthday in May. To add to the excitement in the Porter household, we were delighted with the birth of our third son,

Sigerson, in September. Beyond my life at home with my family, I'm a working mother with a career that I love, surrounded by a team of amazing people who are helping to build our spirited lifestyle and design company—Tracy Porter, Inc.

I share this news with you because even though there are many new happenings going on in my life right now, I still want my home to be my sanctuary. To my delight, my sanctuary has indeed changed over the years. Before my children were born, I was able to spend more time rolling up my sleeves and re-creating a room . . . whatever it took to give my space a new look. Beautifying my home is and will always be a part of who I am. However, now when I need a decorating fix, I choose to do simpler things such as embellishing and repositioning accessories in my space. I also enjoy working around all of my children's essentials, which certainly makes for a fun and creative challenge. Many of the photos in this book were taken before the boys were born. Just try to envision these same photos layered with toys, books, and bouncy seats.

I know throughout my life there will be times again, when I will want to throw my energies toward decorating overhauls. For now, however I'm quite content picking and choosing my projects. In the pages of this book, we hope to share with you inspiring ideas . . . some that are quick, simple, and inexpensive, and some that can be a bit more time-consuming. No matter which stage you're facing in your life, hopefully you will find some inspiration here that tickles your fancy. Surround yourself with loveliness.

From our studio in Wisconsin,
April 2002
Tracy Porter

TRACY PORTER'S

HOME STYLE

How to *dream* with

your eyes open:

Believe in fantasy.

Aspire to *miracles.*

Experience magic.

Savor the journey.

THE TEMPTATION OF *color* AND

combinations

Ah . . . Freedom!

Fuchsia, lilac, ochre, citrus green—beautifully combined with pattern and texture. In the last several years, I've found an even greater love for color and have been able to listen to and feed my soul by enhancing my home with things that I truly love.

We've used as many as fourteen colors on the walls of our home. To some that may seem excessive and even frightening. To us, it is a way to soften the hard lines of a modern, newly built structure. Hopefully, most of these colors I will love for years. However, if

needed, repainting is a chore that my husband, John, doesn't seem to mind when I occasionally ask him to indulge me. He seems unaware that as he paints I stand looking onward . . . so thankful on one hand that he is tackling this job, but on the other hand hoping—*is this the right color?? . . . Oh dear, he's halfway done—will I love it when he's finished?* Yes, we all have these fears! So just remember . . . try to be brave—this is the fun stuff!

Our goal in the following pages is to share with you our vision, which we hope will, in turn, inspire you to look within your own soul to find what feels most comfortable and delightful in your own home.

inspired color

AS A MOTHER, I totally understand how important function is to a home, although sometimes I just need that perfect little something because it's pretty. At left is a terrific example of how something beautiful can also be functional . . . a lovely chair bought for its personality rather than for its intended purpose.

Why not allow something that you adore inspire the colors you choose to live with? In this case, our chair influenced our color choice for the walls. We painted over old textured velvet wallpaper using the same brilliant turquoise blue as this darling little chair to give the walls a new look. We then set off the trim and floors with high-gloss white. Who says you can't paint your woodwork? One of my mantras is: No Rules!

TIP *a fun twist*

Delight your eyes with a simple object perched on the seat of a chair. Here, we chose a ladylike antique pincushion—any treasure certainly will do.

AS ENJOYABLE AS decorating can be, it also has its share of creative challenges. This small home doesn't have an actual dining room. Instead, this corner nook in the kitchen is transformed into the perfect spot for a casual breakfast or an elegant dinner.

The basic structure of this room is rustic, and the woodwork was initially natural just like the floors. We decided to paint the walls a creamy white and the heavy beams a dusty pale blue. This color scheme opens up the room and enhances the natural light from the picture window.

As an enchanting layer, a European glass chandelier and gilded chairs are thrown together in this delightfully casual space. For a luxurious table linen, don't be afraid to use something as unusual as these satin drapes ($12 found at a thrift store)—they take this setting from casual to sophisticated in just seconds. Luxury need not cost a lot to look fabulous.

Consider the different rooms in your home and how you function within them. Maybe you, too, can find a new purpose for one or more of your spaces.

Tracy's Tips for Achieving an
Eclectic, Lived-In Look

An eclectic environment isn't "decorated" with everything in perfect order . . . Instead, favorite things are thrown together to create a lived-in look that is wonderfully personal.

❊   Mix colors, patterns, and textures.

❊   Experiment with a variety of elements and treasures . . . some old, some new, and certainly all that reflect the dear souls who have created such a space. What a great freedom!

❊   An eclectic home is fluid . . . ever-changing. By simply adding or removing an object or two, you might be surprised at how easily your space is transformed. Remember, it's up to you—you're the editor.

❊   Play a game with yourself . . . move one object from each room into another. You'll be delighted with the fresh, new look.

❊   Alternative ways to use things:

- *Bring a birdbath inside as a charming stand for fresh flower arrangements.*

- *Turn an elegant vase into a container for your pens and pencils.*

- *Mismatched goblets become charming candleholders for a centerpiece or on a mantel—a great excuse to buy inexpensive single goblets at flea markets and antique stores. Also a terrific use for goblets that used to be part of a set—if some are broken, use the remaining.*

- *When privacy isn't an issue, exchange one of your interior wooden doors for a light, airy screen door. Hang a sheer curtain on the inside for some wonderful texture.*

ALLOW YOURSELF TO appreciate the beauty of an unmade bed. Sometimes I love the neat-as-a-pin look and other times I can get lost in the precious thoughts of a lazy Saturday morning with John and the babies cozy in our nest. It's the way we love to live . . . a combination of casual, like this bedspread (actually a tablecloth), and formal whimsy, like the lovely curtains and antique bed. Add a backdrop of over-the-top lime green paint with adjacent walls painted a powdery blue, a lovely ochre, and a lively pink. I generally choose not to paint all the walls of a room a single color . . . it makes for a perfectly delicious environment.

A BROWN ANTIQUE mohair sofa is softened with throws that are highly embellished with beading and embroidery. What sets off this combination are the subtle colors of pale blue and champagne against a rich chocolate brown. Perhaps this palette could be the starting point for your next room that needs a makeover.

A CONFIDENT SHADE of red can be the perfect wall color to set off a charming arrangement of your favorite pieces.

❋ Don't be afraid to break up a pair of paintings with a sconce or another decorative treasure as we've done here. Try a mirror, vintage plates, or a shelf in between a pair of paintings.

❋ Consider the number of pieces you want to use and the arrangement of your display. Try hanging your collection vertically, horizontally, or asymmetrically.

THIS EMBROIDERED BEDSPREAD
reminds me of all the needlework my grandmother
used to love so much. It allows me to personalize my
space because it evokes her memory in so many
ways. Go on a treasure hunt for something that
reflects someone who's dear to you. Allow those
memories to live with you every day.

Tracy's Tips for *Personalizing Your Space*

We all love the idea of home because our homes are defined by who we are. Look around your home and ask yourself if enough of your personality shows throughout your space. Allow your home to be one of your creative extensions.

❧ Utilize family pieces handed down from generations, whether it be a piece of furniture, a special lamp, or a wonderful family photo. And don't be afraid to alter or change them (reupholster, paint, or embellish).

❧ Paint a poem along the crown of your favorite room—a pretty stencil or your own freehand creation will add a personal layer.

❧ Your home reflects who you are—don't be afraid to use colors that you love. Have fun and experiment with your paint, fabrics, rugs, and pillows.

❧ Scent is so powerful. Why not select candles that fill your home with a beautiful fragrance? If you have a signature perfume, why not mist your curtains with it? Every time the sun shines or the wind blows through, your home will smell like you.

❧ Bring out things in your decorating that have meaning. Sometimes the most interesting things we own are tucked away in boxes:

- *Old love letters—why not frame them?*
- *Fancy china that only gets pulled out for "special" occasions—life's too short for every day not to be special. Live with it, display it, use it.*
- *Family photos—most everyone has dozens of albums or shoe boxes overflowing with priceless photos . . . Let them personalize your home in groupings or as stand-alone statement pieces. The frames that you choose for them can add a layer of personality —modern, romantic, vintage, simple, or industrial—the possibilities are endless.*
- *Christmas ornaments—pull out some of your non-traditional holiday ornaments such as silvered glass balls, sugared fruits, or even a beaded garland. A touch of sparkle here and there can liven up any vignette.*

    Use them to adorn curtain rods, valances, or even curtain tiebacks.

    A basket or bowl filled with them makes a nostalgic centerpiece for a coffee table.

    A beaded garland can add personality to a fireplace mantel, a chandelier, or even a shelf full of family photos.

JUST LOOK AT the color of these exquisite powdery pink blossoms! I simply had to paint my dining room this color as a great way to add personality to one of our most treasured rituals: gathering for a delicious meal. Is there a particular color that really does it for you? A hue that is absolute candy for the eyes will do. Take a moment to dream about it, and then layer it onto the walls of your favorite gathering spot.

Tracy's Tips for
Embellishing

Throughout this book you'll see many examples of simple everyday items that we've embellished to enhance their personality. You'll be amazed at how fun and addictive this can be!

❁ Favorite goodies to embellish anything and everything:

- *Ribbons and trims*
- *Buttons*
- *Millinery flowers*
- *Shells*
- *Charms*
- *Costume jewelry*
- *Fabric remnants*
- *Wallpaper*
- *Paint*

❁ Simple embellishing can be quick and easy:

- *Add goodies to a lampshade.*
- *Alter a doorknob with decoupage.*
- *Give an old chandelier a facelift—paint it and add ribbons or charms for a new look.*
- *A few specially placed items on a mirror frame may just do the trick.*
- *Add a decorative trim to a rug, pillow, or curtain panel.*
- *Take an ordinary painting or piece of framed art and glue some delicious items onto it.*

❁ More involved "weekend" projects:

- *Take a desk, armoire, or dresser and cover the panels and surfaces with a mix of wallpapers and fabrics.*
- *Paint a wooden chair a new color and add a fanciful fabric cushion to the seat—perhaps tie it on with delicate ribbons and millinery flowers.*
- *Any ordinary door can be embellished with plaster relief to create a one-of-a-kind architectural statement piece.*

MY FRIEND'S OLD desk was originally very bold and colorful, painted red with gold accents. We decided to take this desk and reinvent it, going for a completely charming, old-fashioned feel. By coating it in a high-gloss white paint, then embellishing it by gluing on remnants of a lovely floral fabric, we were able to achieve this new cottage look.

Combined here with a beautiful Venetian glass mirror, our newly created desk is given a delightfully unexpected twist.

Paint can easily change the look of most anything. Imagine this same desk dressed in a coat of high-gloss black lacquer with silver leaf accents!

Think of the possibilities for your own home. They are truly endless!

decorated drawer pulls

AS MUCH AS we love to design something new, the idea of reinventing something we already have is just as exciting. Using inspiration from a favorite theme—in this case, the garden—we've created a variety of decorated drawer pulls and cabinet hardware.

- Use these fanciful pulls to add a special touch to your favorite dresser or armoire.
- Hang four of them on a wall near your vanity—they make a great place to display hair accessories and jewelry.
- Use as a place to hang your goodies on the back of a closet door.

SEE OUR MAKE & CREATE GUIDE ON PAGE 186 FOR INSPIRATION AND BASIC INSTRUCTION ON THIS PROJECT.

creating

MAKING AND CREATING is what our studio is all about! Here's an idea for a tissue box that can add a nice touch to your bathroom or vanity.

SEE OUR MAKE & CREATE GUIDE ON PAGE 187 FOR INSPIRATION AND BASIC INSTRUCTION ON THIS PROJECT.

DRESS UP and add charm to a worn love seat with a simple embellishment. Here we've used a millinery flower and some glass grapes.

If your sofa isn't one for embellishing, why not use this same idea for tablecloths, throws, window treatments, lampshades, or pillows? Experiment!

TIP *collecting embellishments*
Start keeping your own stash of embellishing goodies. Keep them close at hand in baskets or bins for your next impromptu project.

Tracy's Tips for
Color *Inspiration*

Color evokes emotion! Have you ever tried painting your bathroom a brilliant shade of periwinkle? your foyer an inviting tangerine? or your kitchen a shade of sunny yellow? If you haven't, what are you waiting for? Part of the beauty of color is in the exploration. Trust your gut, your heart, and your whims.

Take the intimidation factor out of color. It surrounds us in our world. Draw upon a place where it feels comfortable to you, and it will be easy. Use these familiar sources as your starting point:

- Magazines, art books, photographs, paintings—you name it.
- Textiles—Take a closer look at the colors you are drawn to in your bedding, table linens, and bath towels.
- Environments—Everywhere we go we can pay attention to the colors used to create a delicious mood. Whether it's a restaurant, your favorite store, a friend's home, a museum, or an art gallery, take the time to notice the colors selected to create the individual feeling of the space.
- Nature—Talk about outstanding color! Just think of how many hues exist in the trees, grasses, flowers, gardens, and sky.

When considering all of these wonderful choices, don't limit yourself to applying them only to your wall colors. Think about your home furnishings and decorative accessories as ways to layer in texture, pattern, and other colors. Dream!

THIS IS A great example of a room inspired by rich color. Even though the walls are painted white, the furniture, textiles, and accessories are all layered with shades of burgundy, ochre, greens, and pinks. It goes to show how effortlessly color flows together if you're willing to spend the time experimenting with combinations.

On the following pages, see this same bedroom's makeover.

ROMANCE INSPIRED US
as we chose our palette for this makeover. Lilac walls, a light blue ceiling,
and a thrift store coverlet got us started. The layering-in of unexpected
twists like our headboard, which was
simply wallpapered, a lovely wool rug
borrowed from the dining room, and
a Chinese umbrella used to soften an
overhead ceiling light gave the room
that special eclectic touch. For the holiday season, we added a few festive
accents. A makeover can be as simple
as changing your wall color or as elab-
orate as this top-to-bottom project.

romance

COMBINATIONS OF STYLES are another way to shake up your decorating. If you haven't tried this approach before, bring some unexpected elements together to create a spirited vignette. Think of mixing things from a range of cultures, time periods, styles, and fashions. Here are the ways we mixed styles:

Accessories

❋ **Asian chest**

❋ **Velvet-backed leopard scarf**

❋ **1940s martini set**

Colors

❋ **Red wallpaper**

❋ **Linen-colored baseboards**

❋ **Black high-gloss floors**

A HIGHLY EMBELLISHED piece of furniture can liven up even the most basic of rooms. These decorated chairs, as an example, could add great interest to a dining room by being put at the ends of a table. They could also add charm to a bathroom or interest to a foyer.

SEE OUR MAKE & CREATE GUIDE ON PAGE 188 FOR INSPIRATION AND BASIC INSTRUCTION ON THIS PROJECT.

TIP *Adding Interest to Any Room*

If you like the look of these lively chairs, but a project like this doesn't intrigue you, try to find interesting chairs that have an ornate shape or a fun mix of materials. Many period-style chairs fit this bill. You never know what you may discover.

THIS CLAW FOOT tub is another great example of an unexpected place that can be easily decorated. It now becomes a whimsical addition that would be delightful in any bathroom.

TIP *adding charm to your tub*

Consider freehand painting or stenciling in latex or oil-based paints—or try other embellishments to enhance and add whimsy to your tub.

HERE ARE TWO of many ways in which to view small spaces. Either drench the space top to bottom in a light color to create openness . . . or saturate it with a rich color to create a sense of coziness and warmth.

This cottage kitchen's original makeup was red brick and dark woodwork. While such a combination evoked the comfort of a log cabin, we felt this space yearned for a lighter touch. We opened up the kitchen using white and pastel-colored paints to create a sense of space and airiness.

WE ALL WANT lovely things with which to decorate our walls. Here's one quick, inexpensive option: Keep your eyes open for unframed prints when antiquing, or look to your own favorite books for something to color copy (or if you dare, tear out). The choice to bypass a formal frame will give you a loose, casual feel—à la an artist's studio. Fastening elements to the wall is as simple as using a single decorative upholstery tack. A fanciful button or charm could be added to the tack for an elegant touch.

TIP *color*

Consider choosing colors from prints for your wall color. Here we chose an elegant plum and green combination, as inspired by the wildflowers in the pictures.

THIS CHARMING LITTLE bathroom was painted a cheery fuchsia pink. An unexpected skirt of tulle and velvet trim gives the sink a touch of whimsy. Embellishments such as the crystal trim added onto the light fixture and the wallpapered mirror give this bathroom a unique twist. A playful shower curtain of colorful florals pulls it all together.

Tracy's Tips for
Bathrooms

If you are a person who is intimidated by trying on a new look in your home, a bathroom can be a great place to start. In most cases, bathrooms are the smallest rooms in the house, which generally means less money will be spent on paint, wallpaper, and materials. The impact of a newly decorated room is also more contained, giving you the freedom to feel very brave. So go on . . . what are you waiting for?

- A bathroom makes a great place to use a punchy color or fun wallpaper.

- Make it a personal space for you—bring in some pretty antiques and family photos.

- Colorful rugs add personality.

- Set out stacks and stacks of white towels—pamper yourself!

- Use pretty containers for all of your goodies: bud vases, your children's christening cups, teacups.

- Medicine cabinets are the best. If you don't have one, buy one and hang it over your sink. It's such a great way to hide all the essentials. I truly couldn't live without one! My home currently houses an assortment of cabinets in my bathrooms—from inexpensive basics (found at home improvement centers for around $40) to antique medicine cabinets that simply needed a fresh coat of paint ($15 and up for the paint).

THIS SAME BATHROOM was treated to a makeover with neutral colors and fabrics. Notice how the changes give this room a completely different look. The wooden mirror was painted in cheerful stripes so it would become the focal point of the room. A plaid skirt was attached to the sink with a charming border of silk leaves.

Let nature

inspire you.

Tracy's Tips for *Changing* the Feel of a *Bed*

Allow your bedroom to be a sanctuary, a place for personal comfort. Some of the following touches may inspire you.

✻ Exchange or replace pillows from other rooms to freshen up a tired look.

✻ Mix and match sheets and pillowcases. Pull out different pieces from sets that you have in your linen closet—what an easy way to bring a new color and pattern combination into your bedroom. Additionally, when you are buying new linens, don't feel obligated to get matching sets of everything! If you have several sleeping pillows on your bed, why not buy an assortment of pillowcases?

✻ Warm up your bed in winter with cozy linens in rich colors—in summer, use light fabrics and soft colors.

✻ Give your bed a new personality with a creative headboard:

- *A vintage door mounted to a wall behind your bed horizontally or two mounted vertically is a great way to bring some architecture into your bedroom.*

- *A set of garden gates can add some charm as a headboard. Paint them a fun color, and you'll have something extraordinary.*

- *Paint or wallpaper your current headboard.*

- *Have a piece of Masonite (a thin, dense board) cut to any shape that you desire. (Your local lumberyard or building supply store should be able to do this for you.) Take it to an upholsterer who can pad and cover it with your favorite fabric. If you're a crafty soul, try your hand at upholstering the headboard yourself.*

- *Place an old freestanding fireplace mantel at the head of your bed. Secure it to the wall and upholster the inside of the "opening" with a simple linen fabric. The top of the mantel can be used for all of your essentials—reading lamps, favorite books, alarm clock, etc.*

Bed skirts add a soft layer to any bed. Here are a few simple ideas to transform your existing bed:

- *Bed skirts come in many styles. If you currently have a ruffled bed skirt, why not try one that is refined and tailored? If yours is made of heavy cotton or linen, try a skirt that is sheer.*

- *Sometimes it's fun to change your skirt if you've always kept it the same. For me, I've always been drawn to solid white or cream skirts. I thought it might be fun to add a little pattern to our bed, so I bought a wonderful toile skirt that I just love. Even though it is patterned, the fact that it is classic allows it to coordinate with almost anything that I put on top of my bed.*

- *Even vintage fabric remnants could make an adorable bed skirt when sewn together.*

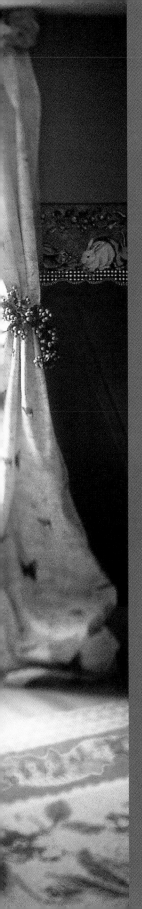

THE STORY HERE is in saturated bright colors and combinations of patterns and textures, from the bold floral cotton bedspread to the silk flowers adorning the top of the window frame. This unusual mix seems to flow magically and creates a most inviting and enchanting bedroom.

On the following pages, see a calming transformation of this lovely room.

THIS TIME WE were inspired to decorate our room in a vintage feel. The subtle colors chosen for the walls and furniture create a backdrop for the quaint mix of elements that were selected.

TIP *themes*

One way to approach decorating is by choosing a theme. Are you inspired by a lovely poem? a favorite season? or even a Broadway musical? If so, allow this theme to influence your decision-making process.

THIS CHOCOLATE BROWN sofa against the painted log wall makes for a striking statement. The unlikely medley of colorful pillows adds yet another dimension to this setting. It's another way to soften an otherwise dramatic vignette.

medley of color

Tracy's Tips for Ways
to Use *Pillows*

Pillows are available in a wide range of colors, patterns, and prices. You can easily create a stylish look quite simply and inexpensively.

※ Don't be afraid to mix styles of pillows . . . they can all work together!

- *Needlepoint*
- *Fabric*
- *Tapestry*
- *Some with ornate trimmings, some without*
- *A range of colors*
- *Old and new*

※ Oversized pillows create extra casual seating around coffee tables and fireplaces.

※ Vintage or good, loose, down–filled throw pillows take a tailored, formal chair or sofa to a more casual place.

※ Things to turn into pillows:

- *Baby blankets*
- *A faded old sundress*
- *Wall tapestries*
- *A large fabric napkin or scarf*
- *Tablecloths*

※ You can never have enough throw pillows . . . so have fun using them in a multitude of ways.

THIS EXOTIC VIGNETTE
was inspired by a variety of cultures.
Often the combination of unique treasures can make for unexpected harmony.

Live with what you love, and the combinations of beautiful vignettes in your
home will be endless.

TIP *functional display*

Recognize this desk from page 16? A
desk creates a sensational display area
for almost any vignette. It adds a touch of
nostalgia to a room whether it actually
serves a functional purpose or not.

Home,

as with life,

is what you make it.

living WITH YOUR *treasures*

Many of us have collections that most people would never see upon entering our homes: silver, china, glassware, our grandmother's lace pieces, postcards . . . What are we waiting for? These nostalgic items could add beautiful layers to our homes. Do we dismiss them because we don't know how they should be displayed, or simply because we haven't taken the time to consider all of these hidden treasures? Perhaps even the collections that we do keep out need some new life, an unusual twist . . . a fresh perspective. Collections are little glimpses into our lives, our history. They tell us

where we've traveled. They speak to our past, our passions, our eclecticism. They even reflect the simple fantasies of who we'd love to be.

I encourage you to open your treasure chests, dig through your attics and basements, and pore through unopened boxes that are buried under a blanket of dust. I once found several yards of fabric that had been buried away for years. As I rediscovered it, I realized what a perfect look it would be as curtains in our guest bedroom. Perhaps in this chapter you will uncover a new way to really live with your favorite things. For you and all those who enter your home, your collections will become a window into your soul.

create a collection

A SMALL COLLECTION of miscellaneous pottery is a simple display in a gardener's shed.

Sometimes it's easy to create a collection just by pulling together various objects of the same color scheme. An old window serves as a lovely and interesting backdrop for this assemblage. Notice too how beautifully it frames the shed's old barn-board walls.

A LOVELY DISPLAY of mixed dinnerware and glassware makes for interesting eye candy. A few unexpected twists thrown in, such as a small glass mirror and vintage figurine, allow for some additional character in this already charming vignette.

ALL OF THE small trinkets in this montage could have easily been thrown into dresser drawers, the bottom of the jewelry chest, or even the toy box. They have happily come together to create a personal collection of miniatures that grace the top of my vanity.

TIP *miniatures to gather*

- Vintage perfume bottles
- Toy blocks
- Single clip-on earrings
- Hat pins
- Brooches
- Old lace scarves

Be inspired to start a new collection . . . or rediscover a collection that has been tucked away.

Surround yourself

with loveliness.

Tracy's Tips for Adding *Charm* to Any *Home*

Old or new . . . what home couldn't use more charm? Don't be afraid to live with what you love. Sometimes the chance combinations are what create charm! For example, years ago I was looking for the perfect "something" to frame as I needed to add a personal touch to a lonely spot on my bathroom wall. I searched through boxes of old papers and mementos and came across a congratulatory letter that had been written to me from my dentist upon my first visit as a young child. I chose this sweet note as a memory that would surely add more charm to my home.

- Create a room or even a shelf full of memories—trinkets, letters, gifts, and photos of all that you hold dear.

- Doesn't charm play upon nostalgia?
  - *Display a collection of your favorite auntie's teacups.*
  - *Frame old postcards that you found in your grandmother's attic. And if you weren't blessed with these simple treasures, find some at an antique store.*
  - *Display a collection that you created as a kid—stamps, coins, or pressed flowers.*

- Allow all of your pretties to be out in your home. Don't hide things in cupboards or in boxes . . . live with them! All who enter your home will appreciate the charm that these items bring.

- Not a big collector? Why not find three big glass jars to display your dog treats on your kitchen countertop? To top each one off, add a metal scoop or an antique spoon as a fun server. Even pets need charm!

- Pull out and display stacks of quilts or handmade blankets that are too beautiful to be stored in your linen closet.

- Use something as whimsical as a nostalgic game from your childhood. Monopoly, checkers, or backgammon displayed on a side table could be charming and playful.

- Try framing your childhood artwork if you were fortunate enough to have kept it.

THIS SMALL CABINET sits on our bedroom window ledge. It contains many beloved treasures that, to me, are priceless. They are pieces of my past . . . old perfume bottles that were my grandmother's, a Valentine from my husband, John, and special family photos.

TIP *evoking personal memories*

Challenge yourself to create a small display such as this that will pull at your heartstrings.

visual appeal

CONSIDER SOME NEW and interesting places to display your favorite things: a dresser top, a bathroom window ledge, or your bedside table. They-may even be things that you use daily . . . you might simply be pulling them together in a fresh way that makes them visually appealing. Displaying a note from a friend or a loved one on your vanity will remind you how loved you are every day. The sweet note you see on my vanity was tied to a Christmas package from some dear friends. I couldn't bear to toss it with the wrappings or store it in a box. I smile every time I read it.

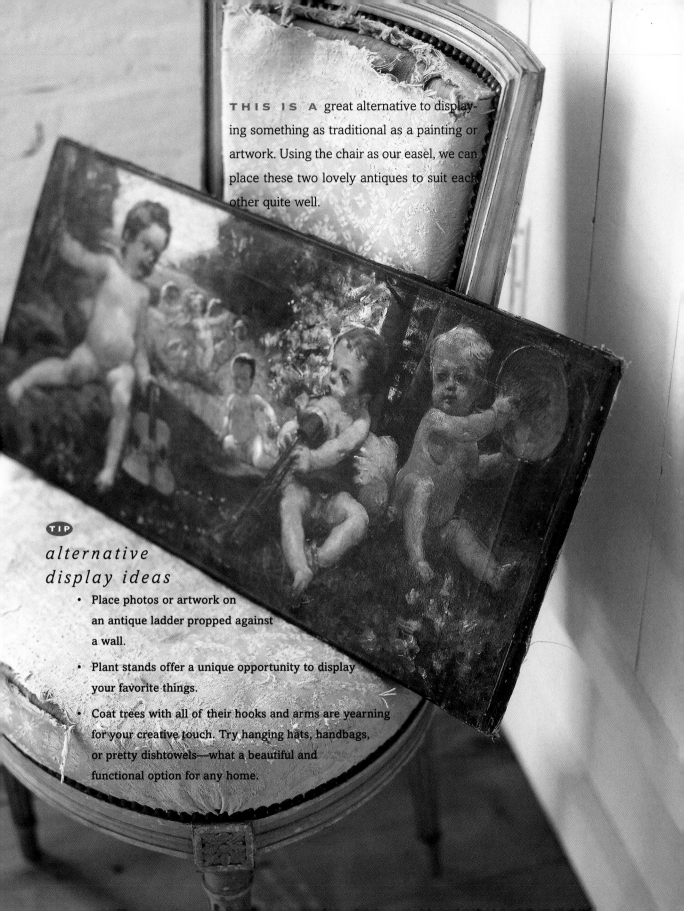

THIS IS A great alternative to displaying something as traditional as a painting or artwork. Using the chair as our easel, we can place these two lovely antiques to suit each other quite well.

TIP

*alternative
display ideas*

- Place photos or artwork on an antique ladder propped against a wall.

- Plant stands offer a unique opportunity to display your favorite things.

- Coat trees with all of their hooks and arms are yearning for your creative touch. Try hanging hats, handbags, or pretty dishtowels—what a beautiful and functional option for any home.

Tracy's Tips for Finding *Things* That Are Timeless

Nothing can be more frustrating in terms of decorating than spending too much money on something that you grow tired of in a few years. Try to take the time to evaluate a piece you're considering. Use the following tips in the process to ensure that you'll love it forever.

- Consider asking yourself questions . . . Is this something you'd still want in 25 years? Is this something you'll want to hand down to future generations?

- Many antiques can be a sure bet. They tend to be more classic . . . or eclectic enough that you'll love them forever.

- Stay away from anything too, too trendy when you're spending money on something expensive like a rug, dining table, couch, bed, chair, or armoire.

- When you're looking at these pieces, make sure you are paying attention to the lines. Will they bother you in 5 years? Are the arms too flirty? Is the back too high? Is the fabric too colorful or fussy? Will it function with your pets or kids?

- Are there things in your home that you live with (and have lived with for some time) that you still love? Determine what clicks with those things and go find new pieces with those characteristics.

I NEVER CAN decide where to live with my garden statuary. Shall I keep it outside . . . or shall I move it inside? Perched on a mantel for the winter and surrounded with fresh flowers from time to time, this delightful little statue will continue to remind me that spring isn't too far away.

USUALLY DISCARDED ITEMS, such as these tin cans, prove that with a little imagination, something so ordinary can serve a new decorative purpose.

TIP *using embellished containers*

- Use as holders for pencils, paintbrushes, and makeup brushes.

- Pot flowers in them, or use as a decorative bud vase.

- Use on your kitchen countertop to hold wooden spoons.

SEE OUR MAKE & CREATE GUIDE ON PAGE 190 FOR INSPIRATION AND BASIC INSTRUCTION ON THIS PROJECT.

Tracy's Tips for Re-creating
Everyday *Things*

There are so many basic items in your world waiting to be embellished. Altered, they could even serve a new purpose—the sky's the limit.

EVERYDAY ITEM	POSSIBLE USE
Pretty envelopes or letters	Wall art
Small dessert plates or teacup saucers	Soap dishes
Shoe boxes	Decorative storage
Old canning jars	Flower vases
An old statue or figurine	An eclectic lamp
A vintage chenille bedspread	A new shower curtain
Ceramic platter or wooden tray	Wall art
Flower pots	Desktop accessories for pens and pencils
Basket	Mail storage
Pretty dish towel	Valance for a small kitchen or bathroom window
Fabric remnants	Sewn into throw pillows or framed as wall art

THESE DECORATED HAND towels can add a whimsical touch to any bathroom or powder room.

SEE OUR MAKE & CREATE GUIDE ON PAGE 191 FOR INSPIRATION AND BASIC INSTRUCTION ON THIS PROJECT.

CANDLEHOLDERS ARE A wonderful thing to collect because you can easily display them together, or set one alone to make a statement. Shown here on a nightstand at the foot of the bed, the placement of this collection of candleholders becomes an unexpected layer in the décor of this bedroom.

BATHROOMS ARE USUALLY places in the house where only the bare necessities are in view. Why not approach your bathrooms with a fresh perspective? Bring in a few of your personal treasures as we've done here.

- Hand-painted wineglasses line the window ledge. A small tea light candle inside allows each glass to serve a new purpose.

- An antique garden gate brings another unusual flair to this space.

- A mix of candles and holders elegantly adorns a wainscoted shelf. The fun of this collection is the variety of heights and the mix of materials . . . even the candle colors themselves are a playful medley.

HAVE YOU EVER considered hanging a beautiful platter on your wall? Ours is hung with a brown velvet ribbon . . . the nail is adorned with an old rhinestone earring glued on its head. Such a small yet whimsical touch can add another layer to your home.

A MISCELLANEOUS COLLECTION of costume jewelry can add a fanciful twist to just about anything!

TIP *decorating with costume jewelry*

- Glue or pin one or a few pieces onto a lampshade.

- Create fancy refrigerator magnets by simply gluing costume jewels onto black magnets.

- If you have a simple picture frame, a rhinestone jewel can be glued on to give it a little sparkle.

- Pin a piece onto a curtain valance or a window-shade pull for a unique touch.

THESE BEAUTIFUL CANDLES may look complicated, but actually can be quite easy to make. One or a few of these on a simple plate or silver tray can add elegant warmth to any room in your home.

SEE OUR MAKE & CREATE GUIDE ON PAGE 192 FOR INSPIRATION AND BASIC INSTRUCTION ON THIS PROJECT.

Tracy's Tips for *Decorating* with *Books*

Books are one of my favorite things in the world. Over the years I have collected so many that I try to use them as an integral part of my decorating whenever I can. To top it off, I've had a fixation with floor-to-ceiling bookshelves in every apartment or home that my husband, John, and I have shared. Now that we have children, I've had to clear off the entire bottom row of our bookshelf, as little fingers were pulling the books out one by one. The books have been replaced with baskets that are overflowing with toys. These books have now found themselves decorating the tops of our tables, our mantel, and even the bathroom vanity. The wonderful thing about books is that they add a layer of personality to most any setting.

- If a book has beautiful interior pages, consider displaying it open in a vignette.
- Use books to elevate statement pieces. For example, a stack of three books with pretty covers makes a great "pedestal" for a grouping of candleholders on top of a table.
- If you have an extra table or top of a buffet, turn it into a minilibrary with stacks of books.
- If you don't have a lot of books and want to decorate with them, consider going to your local library's book sale or even Goodwill.
- Cover your books in fabric or decorative paper if you're looking to create a color statement or a uniform look.
- Put books in unexpected places—on a hall table, on a chair in your foyer, in your dining room, or in a bedroom.
- Why not use books as a headboard? A shelf mounted to the wall displayed with books could be just the ticket.
- When "vignetting" a bookshelf, don't forget to throw other things into the arrangement:

  - *Antiques*
  - *Photos*
  - *Knickknacks*
  - *Ceramic pieces*
  - *Lamps*
  - *Collections*

DIME-STORE GOLDFISH in a pretty glass bowl add a playful touch to this stack of vintage books—a simple and inexpensive twist to any décor.

THE DINING ROOM in our home is graced with a floor-to-ceiling bookshelf (perhaps you read about my fixation earlier). We chose to paint it in a combination of two lighter colors—lovely melon green and a sky blue —hoping to accentuate its architectural lines.

The addition of a richly upholstered oversized chair and a handsome chandelier helps to create a wonderful balance in this setting.

A PETITE, MIRRORED side table is the perfect pedestal for this colorful decanter set. Items such as these can easily be viewed as decorative accessories for your home. Instead of keeping this set tucked away, displaying it allows for beauty and accessibility.

THIS BEAUTIFUL CENTERPIECE inspired by the colors in our linens and dishes makes a marvelous table set for tea. A simple cake stand is the perfect pedestal for a figurine topped with a glass garden cloche and trimmed with fresh flowers.

Tracy's Tips for *Enhancing*
Your Tables

Tables offer the perfect surface for displaying your favorite things. If you aren't sure what to display on your tables, hopefully these tips will encourage your whims to take you to a fresh look in your decorating.

※ Depending on the table, think about the way you are displaying things . . . Are they in rows, in circles, in stacks, or in trays?

※ Coffee tables

- *Try a main statement piece in the center if you use the table often:*

  Garden statuary

  Pot of flowers or topiary

  A big bowl filled with goodies

- *Consider an assortment of lower things:*

  A pretty tray filled with candles

  A runner going across the table with a basket on top

※ Dining tables

- *Nice to have on the table when not in use:*

  A pretty cloche with a small vignette under it

  A row of herbs in small pots

  A cake stand to give height and provide a perfect display piece

  A fresh arrangement of flowers, fruits, or fresh-cut branches

※ Miscellaneous side tables

- *Smaller collections are perfect for these spots:*

  Stacks of books or magazines

  A lamp with a small vignette of photos around it

  A candy dish is always fun!

  Brandies and various decanters with liqueurs

If you need more inexpensive tables . . .

- *Consider buying an inexpensive basic model and covering it with a beautiful table-cloth.*

- *Round barstools draped with fabric work well for a lamp table if space is limited.*

- *A stack of baskets, old suitcases, or even hatboxes can serve as an impromptu table.*

- *Try a garden pedestal with a glass topper.*

character

THIS ANTIQUE MIRROR is a great example of a piece that brings character to a room and also plays a versatile role. For example, a piece like this could serve as a beautiful first layer of a centerpiece. Take the mirror off the wall and lay it on a tabletop. Imagine these possibilities . . . a gathering of candles sitting on the mirror would make a lovely centerpiece—or why not a lovely glass vase, overflowing with flowers and branches? The reflection alone adds to the bounty.

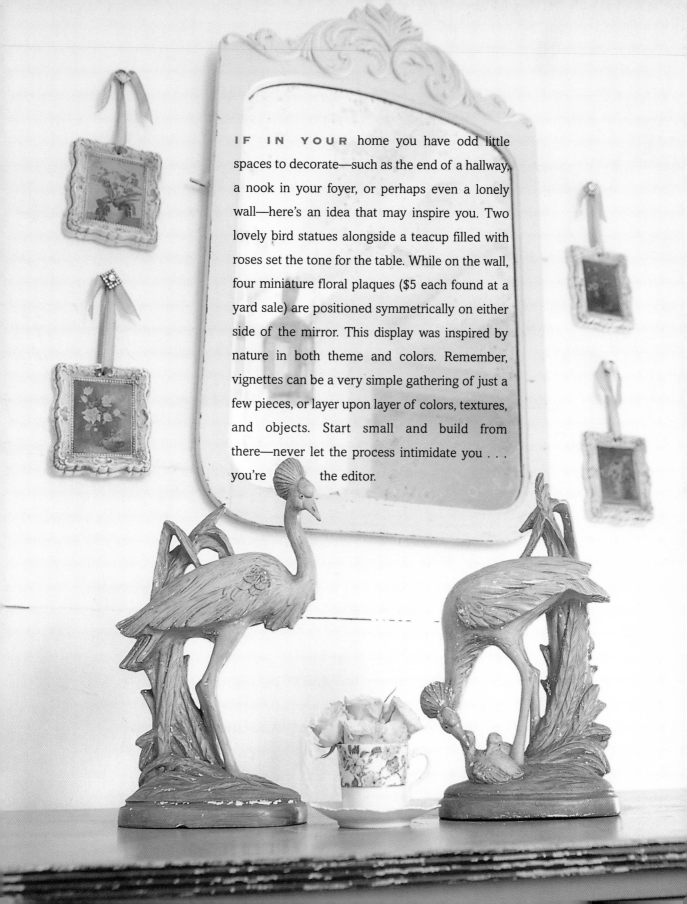

IF IN YOUR home you have odd little spaces to decorate—such as the end of a hallway, a nook in your foyer, or perhaps even a lonely wall—here's an idea that may inspire you. Two lovely bird statues alongside a teacup filled with roses set the tone for the table. While on the wall, four miniature floral plaques ($5 each found at a yard sale) are positioned symmetrically on either side of the mirror. This display was inspired by nature in both theme and colors. Remember, vignettes can be a very simple gathering of just a few pieces, or layer upon layer of colors, textures, and objects. Start small and build from there—never let the process intimidate you . . . you're the editor.

SOMETIMES EVEN MISMATCHED furniture can create an interesting and unique display. The bottom painted antique cabinet is paired with a vintage wall shelf to give us the option of functional storage in both hidden and open display styles. In other words, hide all of your not-so-charming essentials while showing off the good stuff. This is also a terrific example of being resourceful—the cabinet bottom was found at an auction for $45, while the wall shelf was waiting to be discovered at an antique shop for $80. Not a bad ensemble for only $125!

discovering vintage

Tracy's Tips for
Display Ideas

Displaying things is a passion that began for me years ago. Perhaps I was influenced by the environment in which I grew up. In my parents' bedroom, I specifically remember a dresser that had a lovely display of small ceramic figurines, a pair of antique eyeglasses, and a few miscellaneous trinkets. I'm sure memories like these have encouraged me to learn how to live and be creative with all of my own favorite things, rather than simply tucking them away.

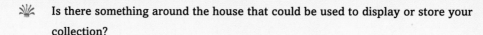 Is there something around the house that could be used to display or store your collection?

- *Use a dressmaker's mannequin to display jewelry or scarves.*

- *Add a shelf below an existing mirror for your collections and put a light above to illuminate them.*

- *Put a shelf above each window in a room—great for vignettes and creating additional space.*

- *Add a plate rail that goes around the top of a room. Think beyond the kitchen . . .*

  Use in the bathroom to display vintage perfume bottles.

  Put one in a kid's room for a train or stuffed animal collection.

- *Why not use a stack of vintage suitcases at the end of your bed?*

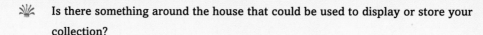 How to use existing things and turn them into great storage or displays:

- *Take wooden fronts off kitchen cabinets and replace them with glass. Show off your essentials.*

- *Use a dysfunctional or off-season fireplace to house your collection of baskets, candles, or other goodies.*

- *Need some unique hooks for display on your doors or walls? Try . . .*

  Antique spoons bent into a U shape

  Several finials in a row

  Glass knobs or pulls

Shadow boxes are a great way to show off the little things you fancy.

- *Try frames for smaller collections or single items such as a pretty key, a leaf, or even a feather found in nature.*

- *If you have a basic shadow box, try adding a decorative molding to the front for added interest.*

- *Alternative shadow boxes: clear glass lamps with removable bottoms, glass garden cloches, antique or new terrariums, or coffee tables with glass tops that house all your goodies beneath. Be creative!*

THE LOVELY DISPLAY in this cabinet is created using similarly colored and decorated dessert sets.

TIP *making a statement*

Sometimes you can create a stronger statement by using treasures that share the same shape and color palette.

THIS ANTIQUE DENTAL CABINET could easily function in almost any room in the house. We've chosen to use it for our "special occasion" glassware. Sometimes it's nice to have an accessible piece with a glass front to display your favorite pieces, while protecting them from the dust bunnies.

Tracy's Tips for *Restyling* an Armoire

One of the most versatile storage pieces we can think of is an armoire. As they come in many shapes, styles, and colors, there's bound to be some way to utilize one or even a few of these in your home. Even if you buy one to serve a specific purpose, just remember that down the road, there are many more possibilities for its use.

※ An armoire makes a great place to store or hide a TV, stereo, clothing, toys, linens, and more.

※ Your home office can be hidden inside.

※ Use one on a sun porch (or in a sunny corner) loaded with potted flowers and your favorite books.

※ Need more storage in your kitchen or pantry? Even a petite armoire can become the most functional tool for you.

※ Remove doors of an armoire to reveal the perfect family photo display gallery.

※ Turn one into a cocktail bar!

※ A small armoire is great in a bathroom stocked with towels and essentials.

※ Tucked into a corner, a small armoire filled with baskets can become a hiding place for all the things you don't know what to do with: camera, photos, video equipment, etc.

※ If your armoire has paneled doors, consider having the panels removed and replaced with brass chicken wire, glass, or a pretty fabric.

※ In a foyer or entry hall, an armoire serves as the perfect place for coats, boots, hats, and more.

EVER CONSIDER A bedside table that also serves as a display piece? This glass-sided cabinet is the perfect answer for all of the essentials you need by your bed.

whimsy

HANDMADE TASSELS SUCH as these can be the perfect addition to any armoire or cabinet. Even the simplest armoire can benefit from a small touch of whimsy.

SEE OUR MAKE & CREATE GUIDE ON PAGE 192 FOR INSPIRATION AND BASIC INSTRUCTION ON THIS PROJECT.

A **SIMPLE SHELF** can serve many purposes—the most important is creating more surfaces on which to display your goodies. As elegant as a single shelf can be, several in a row—either vertically or horizontally—can make a dramatic statement on a wall. Here we've painted and embellished ours to give it additional charm.

SEE OUR MAKE & CREATE GUIDE ON PAGE 193 FOR
INSPIRATION AND BASIC INSTRUCTION ON THIS PROJECT.

Frame a new *photo*

of *loved* ones for

your desk . . . It will

keep a *smile* on

your face all

day long.

ADDING *layers* OF *personality*

So often what really makes a statement is the basic framework of a room or a home. I had an interesting experience in my own home related to this topic. I had this fantasy vision of high-gloss black lacquered floors . . . a grand decorating statement for our new home. Upon the completion of our home-building process, we went ahead and fulfilled my vision throughout the entire house. The floors were absolutely elegant and stunning, just what I wanted . . . until our dogs came into the house, until I came in from the garden, until we tried to clean them, until we tried to function like a normal family with them. We then realized that they were a nightmare. Mind you,

A YOUNG GIRL'S room that houses a lovely arched doorway was the perfect place for us to experiment with embellishment. We chose a pastel-colored tassel trim to line the arch. It draws attention to this beautiful alcove and enhances the already feminine nature of the space. While this idea may be too fussy for most rooms, it was the perfect touch of whimsy for this spirited child's room.

TIP *adding interest to doorways*

It can be fun to view doorways as an extension of your walls. Try on these inspiring ideas:

- Paint your door and the molding that surrounds it a different color than your walls.

- Change or update the hardware on your doors.

- If you have a paneled door, consider painting it a solid color and then wallpapering the panels for added interest.

IF IT SUITS your home's character, try your hand at stenciling initials, florals, or insects as a cameo or border on your wall. We found a stencil that mirrored the beautiful handwork in the antique bed canopy that hangs above our cameo. Sometimes the inspiration for a project can be right in front of you. Dream with your eyes open.

Tracy's Tips for *Enhancing*
Your Walls

Here are some imaginative ways to add some spice to your walls. Some are quite simple—some more complicated . . . All will add personality to any room.

* If you have a room with a chair rail, wallpaper a decorative border along its top edge.

* Discover an unexpected color for your walls.

* Pin or decoupage an arrangement of postcards to your wall to show your personal style.

* Need an unusual and flirty twist? Why not glue wide ribbon onto your wall at chair rail height? If you feel inclined, embellish the top edge with rhinestones, buttons, or seashells.

* If you already have decorative moldings in your home (chair rails, baseboards, crown moldings, door and window frames), try your hand at covering them with wallpaper, fabric, or even decoupage.

* Consider hanging something of sentimental value:
  * *A family quilt*
  * *A framed baptismal gown or other baby clothes*
  * *Diplomas, documents, house drawings, maps*
  * *Children's artwork or even your own from when you were a child*
  * *Your grandmother's old hats*
  * *A group of plates, platters, or teacups*

* Think of doors as a way to alter your home:
  * *Antique doors can add wonderfully unexpected colors and textures to your home. Why not replace some of your existing doors with antique ones?*
  * *Hinge a few vintage doors together for a useful and creative room screen.*
  * *Paint your existing doors a different yet complementary color from your walls.*

FOR A DRAMATIC statement, we decided to use a bold burgundy-and-gold striped wallpaper to accentuate this narrow space that houses a high ceiling. A rug that is colorful, yet muted, naturally suits this space with its inherently organic design. It serves as a wonderful contrast to the severe geometric lines of the wallpaper. For additional flair, a heavy floral drapery was our choice for the window treatments (not what one expects, but certainly a layer that adds an enthusiastic confidence).

A BEAUTIFUL WAY to enhance the simple architecture of a door is by adding character with resin reliefs.

TIP *alternative option*

Looking to create a similar look? Use embossed wallpaper that can be applied and painted any color. It's wonderfully decorative for most any surface.

SEE OUR MAKE & CREATE GUIDE ON PAGE 195 FOR INSPIRATION AND BASIC INSTRUCTION ON THIS PROJECT.

embellish

LOOKING TO DRAW attention to a favorite door in your home? We've embellished our doorknob with bits and bobs to add charm and personality.

SEE OUR MAKE & CREATE GUIDE ON PAGE 195 FOR INSPIRATION AND BASIC INSTRUCTION ON THIS PROJECT.

Tracy's Tips for More *Colorful Floors*

Years ago when we were living in Chicago, I found myself very discontented with the basic white ceramic floor in our bathroom. I proceeded one afternoon to take a hammer and chisel to carve out a 20-inch section in the middle of our floor. Of course that evening, my husband, John, came home to view what looked like a disaster. I, on the other hand, could not have been more thrilled with the fresh clean palette I had just uncovered for my next creation. I spent the next week gluing tiny pieces of glass mosaic tile to create a wonderful floral pattern.

Sitting here today, I look back at myself and the creative energy that I had to pour into that artful project, and I can honestly say . . . it exhausts me. Now that I have a family and a full-time career, I still love attention to detail. However, I now find myself looking for ways to achieve those details through a process that provides more "instant gratification."

The following are quick-fix ideas that can feel timeless and classic and last for years:

- Floors that are worn or covered in smooth materials that you dislike such as linoleum, wood, or concrete can be painted. Experiment with a different palette depending on the room. Brights can be very playful, neutrals always feel classic and easy to live with, and darks can add warmth and elegance.

- Need a temporary fix? Try a variety of scatter or throw rugs. You can mix colors, styles, and construction for a fun, eclectic look.

- If you have a wood or linoleum floor that's in bad shape and you don't want to spend the dollars restoring or replacing it, why not cover it with something other than carpeting? We've tried a heavyweight upholstery fabric fastened down with decorative upholstery tacks. It's a unique treatment that's pretty easy to do. Since you will need to use tacks evenly throughout the floor, choose a fabric that will allow them to blend in, like a plaid, stripe, or all-over motif. This makeover is great for small rooms where there isn't a lot of heavy foot traffic like a bedroom, closet, or home office.

※ Try your hand at embellishing your floor. Consider stencils, decoupage, and different painting techniques. Even a wallpaper border can be used. Simply adhere the paper to a freshly painted or refinished wood floor with wallpaper paste (preferably around the outside border of a room). Once dry, follow up with two coats of water-based polyurethane as a protective sealant on the entire floor.

※ Consider looking at all the rugs in your home and try moving them to other rooms or locations. You may be surprised at how well your bedroom rug works in your dining room.

※ If you've found a tile or stone for your kitchen or bathroom that you would love, but it's too pricey, try using it as a border only. Find a complementary tile that is less expensive for the main coverage.

AN EXCITING WAY to approach a decorating project is to utilize a playful assortment of colors, motifs, and patterns in ways that allow the eye to dance. Here we created a look that feels sophisticated and a bit over-the-top in what was once a simple farmhouse kitchen. To our delight, we chose traditional elements that, when combined in this layered way, feel unexpected yet harmonious.

AH, THE FANTASY black floors from the introduction to this chapter . . . Pretty, aren't they? (To see our floors in a new light, refer to page xii.) Floors like this may very well work for your lifestyle, even though they didn't work for mine. It certainly allows for a beautiful contrast in any room, as it does here, against these pink and lilac walls. No matter what look you choose for your floors, surely it's important to consider your lifestyle.

TIP *mixing styles*

This room gives useful perspective on one way to mix several styles in your decorating. Here, a contemporary metal canopy bed is softened with an antique embroidered bedspread and a cottage-style vintage mirror. A unique velvet valance was created to complement the unusual combination of furnishings that have set an eclectic tone for this room.

EVEN A MUDROOM can use a facelift once in a while. A simple plaid checkerboard pattern was painted on this floor in shades of turquoise. Apricot-colored paper roses were then decoupaged on top. A layer of polyurethane was applied to give this floor a protective coating.

RUGS ARE AN EASY WAY to add your unique style to any room. They're a layer that can easily transform a space, temporarily if needed, and often bring warmth and comfort to your environment. This bedroom's colorful rug playfully coordinates with the floral comforter. The combination of the two gives this room a romantic, cottage feel. Don't be afraid to introduce a variety of patterns into a single space—often the outcome will be even more charming than you had anticipated.

Tracy's Tips for *Interesting* *Window* Treatments

Every room has a unique personality. Enhance the feeling with any of the following ideas. Have fun!

❋ Instead of discarding old scarves, consider what elegant curtains they could make on a small window. Just fold over the top an inch or two and sew or glue. Slide onto a curtain rod.

❋ Any window treatment that's feeling tired to you can benefit from a little quick embellishment. Glue on tiny rhinestones, add a wide band of ribbon, or even try a heat transfer of your favorite image. A wide variety of heat transfer products can be found at any fabric or craft store.

❋ Here are some inexpensive and unique options:

- *Tulle—layer it on for a fluffy, romantic look. It's versatile, easy to work with, and comes in many colors*

- *Felt—a wonderful surface on which to embellish (appliqué, embroidery, or even gluing as an option). A favorite in kids' rooms for a whimsical treatment, or in a bathroom or study for a dramatic, more tailored approach.*

- *Burlap—an inexpensive material that is very easy to drape. It can feel very rustic or totally modern, depending on how you choose to use it.*

❋ Looking for instant charm?

- *Add mullions (wooden window grid inserts that create the look of paned windows).*

- *Use shutters inside.*

- *Try toiles, smaller prints, or ginghams.*

- *Line a window ledge with books.*

- *Put decorative finials on your curtain rods.*

- *Find or create interesting tiebacks.*

- *Try turning an old bedspread into curtains. Chenille or cotton matelassé could be particularly charming.*

KEEP YOUR EYES open for new or antique window treatments that have character. They will surely enhance your style of decorating in any room.

TO ADD A romantic twist to your windows, allow your curtains to puddle on the floor. Consider buying curtains that are longer than your window height to achieve this look.

Tracy's Tips for Finding *Yourself* a Personal Space

One of my favorite personal spaces is the vanity in my bedroom. It's the perfect space for me to keep my girly essentials in order. I love being able to keep my makeup nicely organized, beautiful bottles of perfume displayed, and jewelry tucked away in the dainty drawers . . . all within arms' reach. I'm also nostalgic about this vanity because, as a child, it sat in my parents' bedroom holding my mother's personal essentials.

✦ Turn a quiet corner into your very own private retreat. This can serve one or many purposes:

- *A place to work on your favorite hobby*
- *A writing desk for all your needs*
- *A reading corner for books and magazines*

✦ Many homes have guest bedrooms that are only used a few times a year. Can this space instead become a room for you? What a great home office! If there is space for a daybed, you could use it for both purposes.

✦ Do you have a basement or attic? Add some fresh paint, soft lighting, and a favorite old chair.

✦ A small vanity in your bathroom or bedroom can make for a perfect space, ideal for pampering yourself.

THE CORNER OF an attic becomes the perfect place to nestle a small home office. All the essentials find themselves in unusual yet functional containers such as metal bins, sewing baskets, and planters. These thoughtful touches have allowed this space to feel very personal. An architectural garden gate adds visual interest, while an inexpensive and flirty window treatment softens the bright sunlight that streams through the window.

SEE OUR MAKE & CREATE GUIDE ON PAGE 196 FOR INSPIRATION AND BASIC INSTRUCTION ON THIS PROJECT.

A BIG COMFY chair is placed in front of a lovely set of antique doors adjacent to a sunny window. What a perfect place for a restful afternoon with our cat Spike.

eye-catching

IN OUR MASTER bedroom, we wanted to create a compelling arrangement of doors to hide our closet space. We were lucky enough to stumble upon a matching set of six old, weathered garage doors that suited our needs perfectly. Adding decorative glass knobs to each of the doors created an interesting treatment that is most definitely eye-catching.

TIP *saving dollars*

Sometimes being creative allows you to be thriftier. These recycled doors cost us a fraction of the price of new ones.

I HAVE A warm place in my heart for antique French postcards, as much of my artistry is influenced by my French grandmother. These artful little gems can add a magical touch to nearly any doorknob, hook, or wall on which you may place them. They're simple and enchanting to make!

SEE OUR MAKE & CREATE GUIDE ON PAGE 196 FOR INSPIRATION AND BASIC INSTRUCTION ON THIS PROJECT.

PLEASE COME BACK, *I'm busy dreaming . . .* Perhaps a small handmade sign utilizing remnants of wallpapers, fabrics, and trims can be an enchanting addition to your personal space.

Tracy's Tips for *Softening* a Room

The following simple ideas all have the ability to add comfort and warmth, thus softening any room:

- Add candlelight—tapers, votives, or pillars.

- Try one of these welcoming wall colors: pink, butter yellow, soft green, a warm ivory.

- Texture is a great way to soften a room. Throw blankets and pillows can add a comfortable layer.

- Consider sheer curtain panels as window treatments. As a rule they tend to filter and soften natural light.

- If you're in need of a slipcover and are looking for a casual feel, make sure it's fairly loose and not overly tailored.

- Scatter cotton or wool hooked rugs on the floor. Sisal or other natural-fiber rugs often create a nice soft look as well.

- Adding lots of family photos to a room can add character and personality to any space.

- A layered look encourages a softer feel—by this we mean not too clean, not too perfectly styled.

WHAT A WONDERFUL invitation for a nap! This antique upholstered twin bed works perfectly as a daybed with a mix of assorted pillows that create a comfy backrest. The sheer fabric draped over the head and footboards creates a sense of intimacy.

A FAVORITE OLD chair of mine with feminine gentle curves adds a softness to every room in which I put it. Although it has seen many different homes and
rooms, it always seems to add useful character. Don't be afraid to move the pieces in
your home from room to room. Know that while doing this, the end goal is to create
a sanctuary within each space.

MY HUSBAND, JOHN, and I came across these beautiful antique doors years before we built our home. We bought them as an anniversary gift to ourselves, hoping that they would become front doors to a new home someday. After much deliberation, we realized we'd have to alter the character of them too much to make them functional and weatherproof for our harsh Wisconsin winters. We chose instead to utilize these doors in our kitchen as pantry doors. Their warm appearance gives our industrial-feeling kitchen balance.

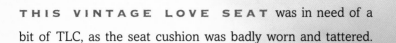

THIS VINTAGE LOVE SEAT was in need of a bit of TLC, as the seat cushion was badly worn and tattered. Our solution was to tuck a velvet throw blanket over the cushion to hide its wear. The textural differences between the upholstery and the throw create a welcoming sense of warmth. Two spirited toile pillows add some life and personality to this comfortable nest.

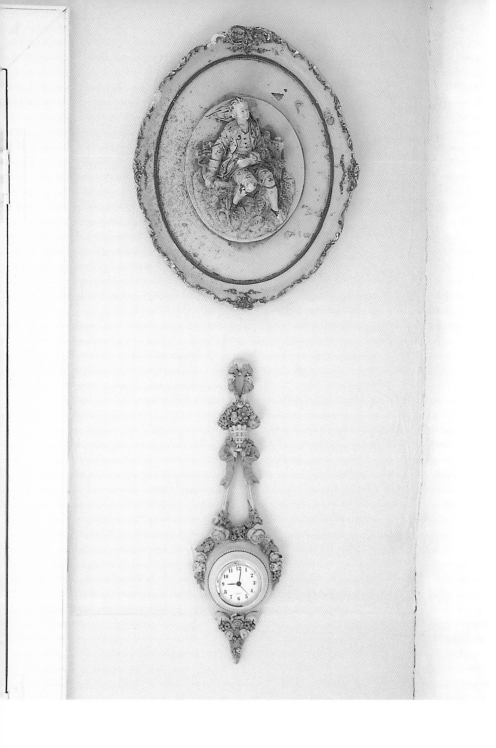

AN ANTIQUE PLASTER relief is paired gracefully
with a small Victorian clock to create an eye-catching vignette.

Tracy's Tips for *Decorating* with Photos

For my husband John's birthday a few years ago, I decided to create a collection of photos as a tribute to his life and the time that we've shared together. Choosing to frame all of them in the same way to create a gallery look also made a wonderful and memory-evoking statement in our home. I can hardly pass by them without stopping to reflect for a moment.

❋ Using the same style of frame will call attention to your wall and create an elegant gallery feel.

❋ Our favorite places for photo arrangements:

- *On a vanity*
- *On a bathroom wall*
- *In a foyer or mudroom*
- *Displayed within your china cabinet*
- *Among the books on your shelves*

❋ Even a less-than-perfect color photo usually looks good in black and white or sepia tone. Your local copy or photo shop should be able to do a high-quality version of your image.

❋ Mix photos in with your favorite collections, utilize as part of a centerpiece, or even tuck one or a few into the corners of your mirror frames.

❋ Create themed stories with groupings of your photos. Birthdays, weddings, anniversaries, family picnics, even photos of your pets can add personality to any wall, shelf, or side table in your home.

❋ Honor your memories. My grandmother used to place tiny little vases with pansies in them next to photos of relatives who lived far away. Flowers and photos can be quite sentimental when displayed together.

AN ARCHITECTURAL MOLDING creates an exquisite surround for a gallery of family photos. Although this is a grand statement, one could just as easily create a compelling mix of photos in a very small space to achieve a similar feel.

A DRAMATIC BACKDROP was achieved by simply hanging velvet curtains on this tiny wall. A wonderful black-and-white photo now holds court without the need for additional wall decorations.

create

AN EASY WAY to further enhance a photo is to create a very personal frame and matting treatment. Ours is embellished with scraps of fabric, silk flowers, and velvet ribbon. Allow yourself the freedom to play with different ideas and materials when thinking about a project like this.

Tracy's Tips for *Living*
with Nature

Exploring nature can offer a useful and inexpensive touch to any environment.

※ When buying holiday greens consider varieties that you can keep out far before and beyond the season. Try myrtle, boxwood, or bay leaf wreaths or garlands.

※ In the spring, keep your eyes open for pretty moss-covered rocks that you can bring inside and use in vignettes. Perhaps you will also discover some abandoned birds' nests or other nature finds that will work with your arrangements.

※ Why not display a big bowl full of lemons for a unique touch to any room? An oversized clear glass hurricane filled with green apples will also delight the eye.

※ When creating pretty flower arrangements, why not try unique color combinations? Who knows . . . it just might inspire your next wall colors.

※ Cut branches add a unique texture to most floral arrangements. They are also beautiful alone in urns next to a fireplace.

※ Embrace the seasons!

- *Spring—Use budding branches.*
- *Summer—Try a colorful bounty of fruits.*
- *Autumn—Collect leaves and dip them in wax to preserve them for months.*
- *Winter—Force bulbs and display them in unusual containers. Perhaps a teapot or interesting cookie jar would be sweet?*

nature indoors

THERE'S NOTHING I like more than finding an excuse to bring the bounty of nature indoors. I always keep my eyes open for interesting containers that can hold flowers, leaves, and branches. This decorative wall pocket was the deal of the century! For a mere three dollars and a coat of paint to cover its former faux gold plastic shell, we turned this garage sale find into something elegant. Freshly cut pink flowers set loosely in this restyled vessel enhance this sophisticated vignette. To add a touch of glamour, a petite jeweled mirror lies just under a cluster of sparkling Christmas ornaments.

TIP *additional uses for Christmas ornaments*

A small cluster of Christmas ornaments could be the perfect decorative touch to hide an unsightly nail head as we've done here.

A NATURE-INSPIRED greeting card sent by a friend finds its home within a hand-painted frame on my wall. Every time I glance at this decorative framed art, I am also reminded of the heartfelt message inside.

Tracy's Tips for *Decorating* Your Mantels

Every once in a while, I need a quick decorating fix. When I get home from work in the evening, I delight in making my children my first priority, and until they go to bed, they are my focus. However, when I can eke out a small amount of time to add a layer to my home, I tend to choose simple and quick ideas. Our mantel serves as a wonderful platform for instant-gratification changes. Below are some of my favorite ideas that I've used over the years that bring attention to this focal point.

- Stacks of books will give a lovely, old library feel when placed on top of your mantel.

- Load up a mantel with framed photos—use various shapes, sizes, and colors. This approach also works well utilizing framed art.

- For a simple and elegant effect, arrange a row of clear glass vases with small ivory candles in each.

- Your mantel is an ideal place for your cherished collections, which are then out of the reach of little fingers.

- A plethora of candles can create a compelling story. Be sure to try various heights, widths, and colors.

- Call attention to your mantel by placing two small lamps on it. This will further enhance the layers of light in your room.

- A useful and particularly charming look is inspired by nature. Try little pots of herbs in a row.

- Accentuate your room by using a central color theme:
  - *A grouping of all white pottery is very classic.*
  - *Aged silver, any shape or size, is an attractive option.*
  - *Black-and-white photos with white matting and black frames can be timeless.*

WALLPAPER CUTOUTS CREATE the backdrop for this newly embellished mantel. The addition of pressed glass decorative flowers, rhinestone buttons, and a small oval plaque complete the fanciful motif.

THIS CHARMING PETITE fireplace adds romance to this bedroom. Even though the fireplace is no longer functioning, it still serves a purpose as a place to burn candles and adds layers of light to this room. Some simple decorative touches give this enchanting piece additional personality.

SEE OUR MAKE & CREATE GUIDE ON PAGE 197 FOR INSPIRATION AND BASIC INSTRUCTION ON THIS PROJECT.

A FAVORITE PLACE of mine is in our great room. I love nothing more than to sit in front of the fireplace and warm my toes. An exquisite antique mirror hanging above this mantel makes a grand statement. I've always loved the old-world feeling that a large mirror paired with a mantel can make. The mantel, both new and inexpensive, needed some embellishing to hold its own next to the beauty of the mirror. Hoping to achieve an eclectic and flirtatious feeling, I was drawn to the kitschy charm of a ceramic plaque, which I then attached to the mantel. Additional layers of seashells and ceramic roses were added to complete this playful look.

TIP *keeping your mind open*

I'm a big believer in looking for creative and cost-effective decorating solutions whenever I can. Spend money on the "to die for" pieces and be penny-wise on the basics. If you feel inspired to embellish your basics, like I did with this $100 mantel, then let your creative hand guide you. Otherwise just let your basics be as they are. Simple and unadorned solutions can bring balance too.

SHOWN HERE IS a beautiful close-up of the intricately embellished detail on the fireplace mantel.

SEE OUR MAKE & CREATE GUIDE ON PAGE 198 FOR INSPIRATION AND BASIC INSTRUCTION ON THIS PROJECT.

Tracy's Tips for *Creating* Order

As much as I like a looseness and "thrown together" feeling in most of my home, there's nothing I love more than wrapping my arms around the order of essentials found in all of my rooms. For instance, flipping through a magazine one day, I was inspired by a fashion editor's closet. I have since then organized all of my dress shoes in attractive boxes that are nicely labeled with the shoe's style. Now when I open my closet doors, I'm inspired by the fresh and orderly view.

※ Discovering similarity among your collections can create a wonderful visual harmony. Try taking this approach when looking for objects to display together, such as color, motif, or even size.

※ Accommodate your essentials with pretty containers.

- *Bathroom:*

   Keep Q-Tips in teacups or silver baby cups.

   Put soaps on an antique silver tray.

   Place toilet paper in a cute basket or box.

- *Kitchen:*

   For wooden spoons and utensils, utilize vases, pitchers, or cachepots.

   Place your phone or answering machine in a square or rectangular storage basket—add a pad of paper and pencils.

   For keys, change, and miscellaneous pocket stuff, create a small basket or bin where each person can organize these daily essentials.

- *Home office:*

   Keep your essentials in decorative hatboxes, old canning jars, or even pretty flowerpots.

   Small fabric-lined baskets are a charming place for miscellaneous papers and mail.

※ Rows of hooks on a wall or inside a closet door create order and additional useful space.

※ In your mudroom or entryway it's easy for clutter to accumulate. To encourage order, try a locker or shelf space designated for each family member.

※ When keeping magazines and books out on a coffee table, consider putting groups of them in trays. This will keep them orderly and easy to access.

appealing

A SIMPLE WOODEN box proves to be a wonderful surface for embellishments as well as an appealing place to store all of your goodies.

SEE OUR MAKE & CREATE GUIDE ON PAGE 199 FOR INSPIRATION AND BASIC INSTRUCTION ON THIS PROJECT.

OUR SOLUTION FOR linen storage in my tiny farmhouse hallway was to utilize this hand-painted wardrobe, which used to house nothing more than a hanging bar. A piece like this can be functional in a lot of ways. If you own a similar hutch or armoire, consider having it outfitted with more shelves or drawers to make it more useful for your particular needs.

functional

The following pages show many delicious examples of how to live with light. We've highlighted many playful and inexpensive ideas throughout this chapter. Our hope is that you'll find inspiration all around you.

layer of whimsy

CONSIDER LOOKING AT any lighting fixture in your home to serve more than just a functional purpose. This vintage chandelier adds a wonderful layer of whimsy to this bedroom. We added these darling shades to soften the light.

TAKING ADVANTAGE OF natural light is essential, especially in a small space. This attic bedroom has a sunny south-facing window, the perfect spot for a vanity. To add character to the window and vanity top, we used nothing more than fabric and trim remnants. No sewing here, simply a touch of glue. Notice the unusual containers that house our flowers and Q-Tips. Don't forget to keep your eyes open for spirited pieces like these that will bring you joy every day.

TIP *added function*

Consider adding a piece of glass to a fabric-covered vanity or dresser top. It will protect the vanity for years.

Tracy's Tips for Adding *Layers* of Light to Your *Home*

❋ Most rooms can benefit from layers of soft light. Try a combination of . . .

- *Overhead lighting*
- *Lamps*
- *Sconces*
- *Candlelight*

❋ There's not a room in the house that doesn't need at least one lamp! Lamps have a way of softening the light if your only source is an overhead fixture. Have you tried one in these rooms yet?

- *Bathroom*
- *Kitchen*
- *Dining Room*
- *Foyer*
- *Children's room*

❋ Nighttime is a great test for how your lighting is or isn't working. Try this easy way to experiment:

- *Buy yourself plenty of bulbs in all wattages from 15 watts up to 100 watts. Simply changing the watts or even the color of a bulb can enhance the feel of light in a particular room. Many interior bulbs now come in a range of pastels like soft pink, peach, and yellow, which can add warmth to a room . . . or pale green, blue, and lavender, which can add a cool cast where you need it.*

❋ Torchères are great options where floor lamps are normally used. With torchères, light is projected up toward the ceiling to create interest.

Curl up with hot chocolate,

a warm fire, and a

good book.

FIREPLACES AND MANTELS are a great place to explore layers of light. Here we've utilized a combination of sconces, firelight (yes, this is indeed a gas fireplace), and candles to create a sense of softness and depth in this room. A light-colored ceiling also plays a role, as it balances out the dark wood floors.

TIP *gas fireplaces are just as beautiful!*

As a reformed fireplace purist (never before would I have dreamed of living with anything but an authentic wood-burning fireplace), I now welcome the chance to enjoy the beauty of a fire by simply flipping a switch to turn on the gas. This is one more lesson that I've learned in the process of simplifying my life.

HERE WE'VE HUNG unusual crystals in a window—they add a touch of color and sparkle to any space. These lovely gems can also be hung from chandeliers, sconces, or even lampshades. We've embellished a few to show you their fancier side.

SEE OUR MAKE & CREATE GUIDE ON PAGE 201 FOR INSPIRATION AND BASIC INSTRUCTION ON THIS PROJECT.

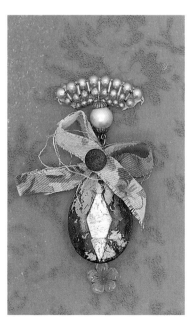

OUR DECEPTIVELY LARGE urban style kitchen was a wonderful exercise in combining unique elements with basic function. Even though we craved a taste of industrial design in this room, we couldn't help but mix in unusual antique architectural elements such as the cornices over the windows and the grand pantry doors, both of which were found through salvage resources. Antique flocked wallpaper and oversize white tiles inspired by French pastry shops add yet another eclectic twist in our kitchen. As with anything in life, the lesson is all about balance. In creating this room, we knew there was a limited budget with which we had to work, so we splurged only on certain things such as the doors, the stainless refrigerator, and the beautiful tile. In turn, we saved ourselves plenty by being creative about the other essentials such as the countertops, cabinetry, lighting, and even the salvaged sink. It can take a little more resourcefulness, but the results are well worth the effort.

TIP *allowing reflective surfaces to work for you*

Notice how the many reflective surfaces allow the natural light to flow easily throughout this space. The combination of glass, high-gloss floors, stainless steel countertops, and white tiles has allowed us to take advantage of the light in the space.

THE NATURAL LIGHT in this bedroom complements the warm soft light of the bedside lamp. A lively pink wall adds a romantic and elegant tone to the overall feel of the room.

I **LOVE TO** use glass in decorating. Whether I'm using mirrors, chandeliers, or beautiful goblets, I always find that the reflective nature of glass brings more light into each room.

Tracy's Tips for *Interesting* Statement Pieces

A great statement piece can be the foundation for a room's personality. We've created a small list of some of our favorites . . . you just never know what you may find.

- Unusual mirrors
- Odd little side tables
- Chandeliers, sconces, candelabras
- Fanciful lamps
- Art for the walls
- Garden statuary—great for centerpieces, or even next to the fireplace
- Ceramic pitchers and platters—nice stand-alones, or beautiful grouped together
- Architectural elements—old doors, cornices, finials
- A great rug
- Decorative hardware for cabinets, drawers, and doors
- A charming armoire
- A vintage mantelpiece
- Pretty window treatments, drapes, curtains, sheers
- Books—a wonderful way to add color and character to a space
- Ottomans—they come in a variety of shapes and sizes

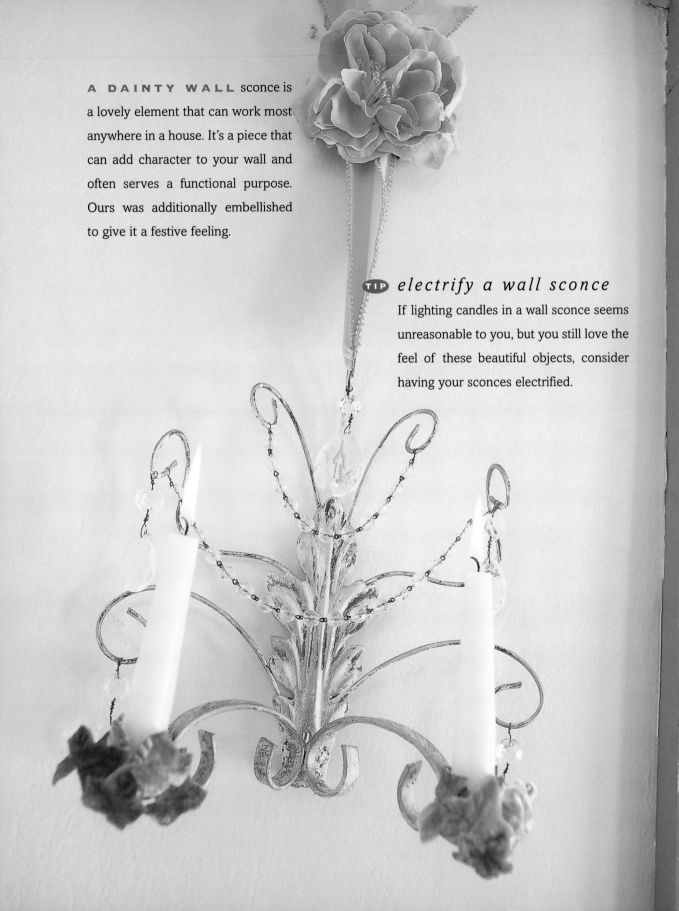

A DAINTY WALL sconce is a lovely element that can work most anywhere in a house. It's a piece that can add character to your wall and often serves a functional purpose. Ours was additionally embellished to give it a festive feeling.

TIP *electrify a wall sconce*

If lighting candles in a wall sconce seems unreasonable to you, but you still love the feel of these beautiful objects, consider having your sconces electrified.

THIS CHARMING DRESSER was originally just an ordinary raw pine piece. Having a need in this bedroom for a beautiful and functional statement piece encouraged us to paint, stencil, and add fanciful glass knobs. The wonderful thing about statement pieces is that they can very often be right in front of your very eyes. Sometimes all they need is a quick makeover.

The cool, soft light in this room was created by using a mix of pastel colors along with lovely sheer panels on the windows, which diffuse the strong natural light coming in. The addition of two petite lamps adds a touch of warmth to this inviting space.

TIP *creative wall art*

In need of a special and inexpensive little something for your wall? Here we simply framed a toile fabric remnant. Dare yourself to dream up a few combinations for your own walls.

INTERIOR DOORS CAN be so heavy and dark. In this space we chose a vintage screen door to allow the light to transfer easily from one room to the other. The curtain panels allow for privacy when necessary. Try using a screen door such as this in your pantry, between the kitchen and dining room, as an entrance into your sunroom, or on a closet with sheer curtain panels behind it.

THIS PIECE OF garden statuary adds an element of old-world charm to our home in the winter. You may have a piece in your own garden that can add a non-traditional twist to any room.

Tracy's Tips for *Decorating* with Mirrors

I love the effects that a beautiful mirror can have on a room. A mirror can add personality and lend a feeling of depth to most any space. A few years ago for Valentine's Day my husband, John, surprised me with a wonderful gift of an exquisite mirror. I treasure this piece and have loved moving it from room to room over the years. It continues to surprise me as it transforms each new space in which I put it.

I love having mirrors in just about every room in my home for the added character and additional light that they draw into each space. The following ideas are ones that I've found to be creative and quite cost effective:

- Find a beautiful frame, old or new, and have a piece of mirror glass dropped in.

- Embellish an existing mirror with old costume jewels, millinery flowers, or even lengths of ribbon for a hand-touched look.

- Rather than a "grouping" of art on a wall, try a gallery of mirrors to create the illusion of a larger space.

- To create the look of a "more is more" space, line the back of a hutch or bookshelf with mirrored glass. This also adds unexpected light.

- Consider putting a mirror where you normally wouldn't:

  - *In a kitchen*
  - *On a door*
  - *Lay one flat on a table for an unusual base for a vignette—build up from there!*
  - *Behind a bookshelf to create depth*

THE COMBINATION OF this unusual pressed-tin mirror and the retro-inspired electric sconces makes for an eye-catching vignette. The sconce cords are simply camouflaged with an elegant piece of silk ribbon. Paired with this petite vanity, this mix of elements is wonderfully eclectic.

AN EXQUISITE STATEMENT piece such as this mirror might ordinarily find itself safely hung above a fireplace mantel. However, the beautiful light that streams into this bathroom yearned for a place to be captured. What an interesting effect this ornate mirror and simple sink creates! Don't be afraid to combine an over-the-top piece that you may own with something plain and simple. The harmony is sometimes a sweet perfection.

THIS GUEST BEDROOM evokes a sense of warmth, light, and depth. Original to this space, the vintage wallpaper creates a warm and highly decorated backdrop, which is set off by the simple lines of this classic twin bed headboard, upholstered in a richly colored velvet. The clean white matelessé coverlet brings light and openness to this tiny space. A brightly colored medley of pillows provides an unexpected and delightful treat for the eye. A dainty gilded mirror tops it off like frosting on a cake.

Tracy's Tips for *Interesting* Ways to Use Candles

I try to view candles as an essential part of my every day. This isn't something that I've always done, but it certainly became a daily ritual once I started. Here are a few of my favorite ideas to encourage you to utilize this wonderful source of warmth in your home.

- Sprinkle votives all over your dining table for your next dinner party.

- Keep a candle or two in the kitchen for added soft light and fragrance.

- For an additional decorative touch, try a grouping of candles on the mantel above your fireplace. The glow will project upward, creating a softness in your room.

- A row of teacups on a coffee table or on a mantel filled with tea lights can add some great warm light.

- An off-season fireplace can be a great place to set a grouping of candles to create some romance.

- When using taper candles, don't be afraid to use several colors in a grouping. For instance, a range of pastel candles in a candelabra could be very magical.

- Use unusual containers to put candles on or in:
  - *Dessert plates*
  - *Large clear vases*
  - *Terra cotta pots*
  - *Decorative coasters*
  - *Goblets*
  - *Pretty bowls*

A SPLENDID MIX of candleholders in various heights, shapes, and colors is a feast for the senses. Nestled comfortably in a deep windowsill, this gathering makes for a statement that draws you in.

TIP *safe ways to use candles*

As much as we love the warmth and beauty of soft candlelight in our home, we always encourage common sense. Never leave a burning candle unattended, especially in the presence of young children or pets. Avoid placing lit candles in baskets or other potentially flammable containers. There are so many safe and wonderful ways to display candles that you should easily find several that fit your lifestyle.

THIS LIGHTLY EMBELLISHED wooden candleholder provides a decorative base for a simple pillar candle.

SEE OUR MAKE & CREATE GUIDE ON PAGE 202 FOR INSPIRATION AND BASIC INSTRUCTION ON THIS PROJECT.

embellish

AN ENCHANTING WAY to draw light into an intimate space is to use a mirror as a decorative base for a centerpiece. Paired with twinkling votive candles that allow the light to dance, this magical ensemble delights the soul.

PLAYFULLY COLORED TAPER candles give these sophisticated candelabras a softer, more casual feel. As they frame this petite fireplace and allow it to feel grand, the collection of memory-filled artifacts hung above help to create an inviting space.

Tracy's Tips for *Reinventing* Lamps

Since my childhood, I've always been drawn to a special piece in my grandmother's home—a large and beautiful alabaster vase that she had turned into a torchère for her table (a version of a lamp that allows the light to shine up without a shade). I now appreciate this unique and lovely piece, not only for the way in which Grandma Lucy transformed it, but also for the function that it now serves. Perhaps some of the following ideas will encourage you to look at lighting in a fresh, new way.

* Change your lampshade—either buy a new one or exchange shades from an existing lamp in your home.

* Consider painting your lamp top to bottom in a fanciful new color. Additionally, try freehand or stenciled painting for a fun touch.

* Add character to your lamp by placing it upon:

  * *A hatbox*
  * *A decorative plate or platter*
  * *A stack of books*
  * *A small mirror to reflect the light*

* Embellish or decorate your lamp by adding unique elements:

  * *Add hanging crystals to the bottom edge of the shade, and possibly to the lamp base or wherever it allows.*
  * *Add flowers and ribbons to soften the look of your lamp.*
  * *Apply a fine mist of spray adhesive to your shade, and then a dusting of fine glitter to add an elegant shimmer.*

* Lamps take on a whole new look when simply moved to a new location in your home.

* A lamp's ability to go from bright to dim can be easily achieved by adding a dimmer switch to the cord. This will enhance the lamp's versatility.

* Add a decorative finial to the top of a lamp's harp. This simple addition can make any ordinary lamp extraordinary.

* Another option is to purchase a wire lampshade frame and start from scratch. This way you can cover it with whatever your heart desires.

EMBELLISHING YOUR LAMPSHADES is an easy and inexpensive way to bring new life to any lamp in your home.

SEE OUR MAKE & CREATE GUIDE ON PAGE 203 FOR INSPIRATION AND BASIC INSTRUCTION ON THIS PROJECT.

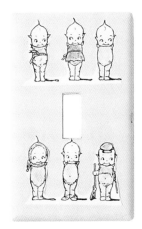

DECORATING INEXPENSIVE OBJECTS, like these switch plates, can make them the perfect addition to any décor.

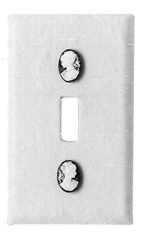

SEE OUR MAKE & CREATE GUIDE ON PAGE 204 FOR INSPIRATION AND BASIC INSTRUCTION ON THIS PROJECT.

OFTEN OLDER HOMES
have windows of unusual sizes. This exceptionally narrow window receives additional width with the help of curtains that are hung just outside of the window's frame, allowing more of the natural light to shine in. The placement of the curtains deceives the eye just enough that you view the window as being grand. This just might be the trick you need for any window in your home.

Tracy's Tips for *Unexpected Places* to Hang a Chandelier

Years ago, I was at an auction with my parents and a dainty little chandelier came up as the next item for bid. I had secretly been admiring this lovely jewel all evening, knowing that it was a piece that I would love to own. Out of the corner of my eye, I saw my father raising his paddle to bid on this item. As he won the bid, I cheered him on—not knowing that his intentions were heartfelt, as he then told me it was a gift for our new farmhouse.

As you can see, I have a soft spot in my heart for my dad . . . and chandeliers. Here are several unexpected places to hang your beloved treasures:

- Over your bathtub
- In the corner of your living room
- In your bedroom
- In a nursery or child's room
- In a hallway—try hanging two or three mini chandeliers in a row
- In the kitchen above your sink
- On a porch

A TINY ATTIC room fit for a princess was the perfect place to host this fairy-tale chandelier. It brings additional magic to this already enchanting space.

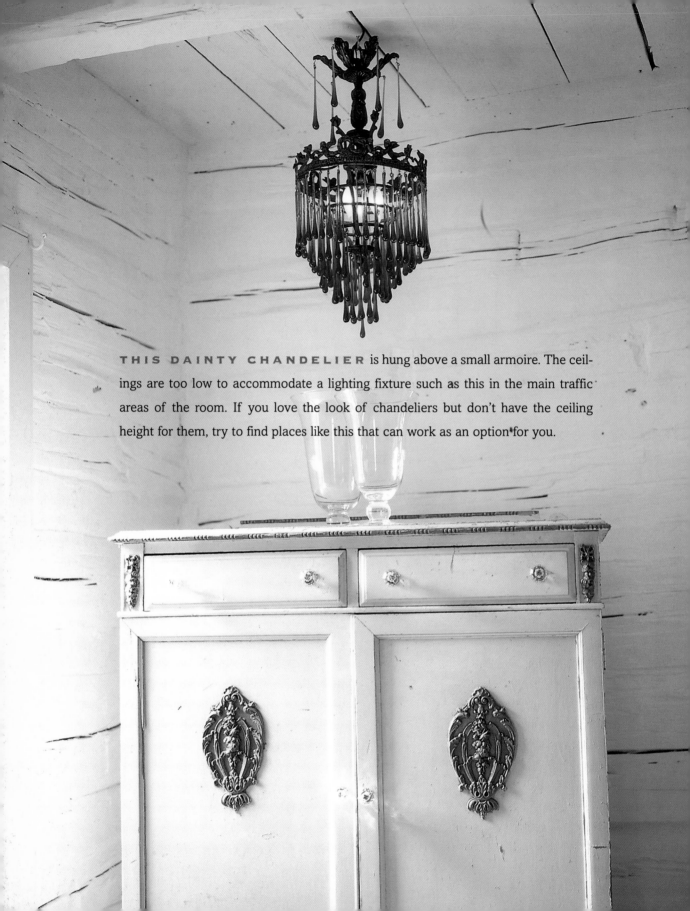

THIS DAINTY CHANDELIER is hung above a small armoire. The ceilings are too low to accommodate a lighting fixture such as this in the main traffic areas of the room. If you love the look of chandeliers but don't have the ceiling height for them, try to find places like this that can work as an option for you.

AN UNCONVENTIONAL BATHROOM gets an added twist from a porcelain storybook-looking chandelier. A panel of vibrant green wallpaper adds to the playfulness of this already delightful space.

TIP *adding fantasy to chandeliers*

Can any of your own chandeliers use a layer of ribbons, crystals, or millinery flowers? Not only a fun project, but sure to tickle your soul.

WHEN HANGING A grand chandelier such as this, consider the space in which it is being displayed. Here, we've chosen a white dining table as an anchor for this statement. It allows the eye to feel balance, while still giving the feeling of dramatic flair.

TIP *creating a whimsical dining statement*
Use a mix of chairs around your dining or kitchen table. This will allow your room to feel eclectic and full of personality.

feel balance

A TRUE STATEMENT piece! This colored glass chandelier can take any room from ordinary to fabulous. While not something that you'll see at every local lighting shop, you can find wonderful chandeliers such as this at antique shops and many specialty stores.

TRACY PORTER MAKE & CREATE GUIDE

projects taken from The Temptation of

Color and Combinations (pages 3–48)

How about getting a pretty new

bowl for your pet to drink

water from? Who says

dogs are color-blind!

MAKE & CREATE DRAWER PULLS
FROM PAGE 17

Decorate an assortment of vintage and new pulls, in a
mix of materials ranging from wood to ceramic.

FABRIC-COVERED

SUPPLIES: pencil ✳ fabric remnants ✳ ruler ✳
scissors ✳ fabric glue ✳ embellishments

- Trace the shape of the knob with a pencil onto the back side of your fabric.

- Measure the depth of the hardware with a ruler, and extend the tracing line of
the fabric by that dimension (i.e., if the pull hardware is 2" deep, add 2" to the
circumference of your original tracing line).

- Cut fabric—center pull on backside of fabric.

- Apply fabric glue to fabric—adhere evenly over the surface of the pull.

- For our garden variety, we used a touch of silk and re-created petals of flowers
using a rhinestone button.

- Plastic berries can also lend a fruity element to the theme.

PAINTED

SUPPLIES: latex, enamel, or spray paint ✳ brushes ✳ stickers ✳ stencils ✳
clear matte finishing spray

- A raw wood knob is easily transformed with a wash of color using paint, brush,
and stickers. Why not try stickers in a selection of garden creatures such as butterflies, birds, and bees? Stenciling or hand painting could also achieve a similar
look.

- When finished, protect your pull with a clear coat of matte finishing spray.

EMBELLISHED

SUPPLIES: hot-glue gun ✳ buttons ✳ millinery flowers ✳ beads

- Drawer pulls, knobs, or cabinet hardware that already have some character are
an ideal selection for this project. We chose fanciful jewel-cut resin knobs as
well as simple wood pulls for ours. Using a glue gun, adhere buttons, millinery
flowers, and beads to create an assortment of floral-inspired designs.

TIP *remember, it's the mix, not the match!*
Don't be afraid to add a variety of your newly transformed knobs and pulls to your
favorite dresser, armoire, vanity, and more!

MAKE & CREATE TISSUE BOX COVER
FROM PAGE 18

Transform a plain wooden, ceramic, or plastic tissue box cover with our step-by-step instructions!

SUPPLIES: fine sandpaper ✳ latex or enamel paint ✳ paint brushes ✳ gift wrap ✳ ruler ✳ pencil ✳ scissors ✳ spray adhesive ✳ satin ribbon ✳ hot-glue gun ✳ clear water-based polyurethane

- Lightly sand the surface of the tissue box cover.

- Basecoat the exterior in your favorite hue—here we've chosen a delicious minty blue-green. Let dry. Apply a second coat if desired.

- To determine the length of the decorative strip (gift wrap or other decorative paper), measure the width of the top plus twice the height of the box. Add at least 1" on either side for folding underneath and gluing in place. For the width of the strip, allow about ³⁄₄" to extend beyond the oblong tissue opening.

- With a pencil trace the size of the oval tissue opening. Transfer this oval shape onto the center of the wrong side of the decorative strip. Lightly fold the strip in half and using a sharp pair of scissors, snip a ¹⁄₂" slit. From this slit, cut triangles just up to the oval outline. (These triangles will be tucked inside the opening and glued to the underside to help hold the strip in place.)

- Apply a thin, even coat of spray adhesive to the wrong side of the gift wrap. Adhere evenly to the surface of the tissue box cover, being sure to tuck under the triangles in the opening and the 1" folds along the two sides.

- Trim three lengths of contrasting satin ribbon—two for the sides and one for the inside rim of the oval opening. (For the inside rim, allow about ¹⁄₂" to overlap—trim on an angle to prevent fraying. For the sides, be sure to add about 1" to each end to allow for tucking inside.) Glue in place using a hot-glue gun.

- To finish and protect your new tissue box cover, apply an even coat of clear water-based polyurethane.

Try substituting wallpaper or fabric remnants for the decorative strip. Or why not try this—simply paint a second color strip and use stencils or freehand painting to gain a similar look. Let your imagination be your guide!

MAKE & CREATE SEAT OF ENVY CHAIRS

FROM PAGES 26–27

Create your own "seats of envy" by giving tired old wooden chairs a colorful and refreshing facelift.

SUPPLIES: wooden chairs (any style) ✻ sandpaper ✻ primer ✻ latex or enamel paint in a variety of colors ✻ brushes ✻ masking tape ✻ stencils ✻ wallpaper ✻ fabric remnants ✻ stickers ✻ spray adhesive ✻ clear water-based polyurethane

- Lightly sand the surface of your chair. Prime if necessary. (If your chair is already heavily painted or varnished, it can be stripped or heavily sanded before beginning painting, depending on the look you want to achieve.)

- Plan out the basic palette of your masterpiece, or experiment as you go . . . Simply think of your chair as a blank canvas. Don't be afraid to paint each leg a different color, and the seat another! Use masking tape to help create lines and borders where there are none.

- Use a variety of stencils, wallpaper, fabric remnants, stickers, and more to add a layer of whimsy to your chair. Adhere wallpaper or other swatches in place using spray adhesive. (Spraying adhesive on both the chair and the wrong side of the swatch will create a longer-lasting bond.)

- Once you are satisfied with the look of your newest creation, seal and protect your chair with an even coat of clear polyurethane.

Try this technique on a variety of other painted surfaces—toy chests, benches, desks, and more . . . The possibilities are truly endless!

TRACY PORTER MAKE & CREATE GUIDE

projects taken from *Living with*

Your Treasures (pages 49–92)

Make a conscious decision to live

for each moment . . . to savor each

day . . . to delight in every person

that is a part of your world.

MAKE & CREATE EMBELLISHED CONTAINERS
FROM PAGE 62

Recycle your old tin cans in a fun new way . . . With just a few simple steps, you can create lovely containers that are perfect for any home office, bathroom, or dressing table.

SUPPLIES: ruler ✳ scissors ✳ tissue paper ✳ an assortment of tin cans ✳ metal file (optional) ✳ gold paper ✳ spray adhesive ✳ hot-glue gun ✳ fabric trim ✳ wallpaper ✳ spray paint ✳ clear glitter ✳ embellishments

A This little soup can was covered using a scrap of decorative tissue paper that we saved from a gift bag.

- With a ruler, measure and then cut a rectangle of tissue paper so that the width equals the height of the can. Wrap the paper around the can to determine the length. Trim the paper, leaving approximately ½" overlap in the back to glue in place.

- The edge where the lid is removed is sharp, so to prevent little nicks, we covered the top edge with a double thickness of gold paper. Fold and wrap around both the inside and outside of the can to form a decorative border. Glue in place using spray adhesive or a hot-glue gun.

- Finally, cut a piece of lovely fabric trim to length and attach it to the rim using a hot-glue gun. Who wouldn't want to put their everyday goodies in something so adorable?

B We used white and yellow vintage wallpaper to cover this slightly larger can. You could also use fabric remnants—whatever you have at your fingertips!

- Allow an extra inch on the height to wrap inside to cover the sharp edge. Adhere using spray adhesive.

- Cut two equal lengths of white lace trim and attach using a hot-glue gun to give this item an elegant finishing touch.

C If "cutting and pasting" isn't your thing, try this simple painting technique.

- Before painting this small can, use a metal file to remove any sharp edges along the inside. You could also run a bead of hot glue along the edge to cover the rough edges.

- Spray paint the can inside and out using your favorite color—here we've used light blue enamel.

- While the paint is still tacky, sprinkle the entire surface with a dash of clear glitter to give this gem a little sparkle.

- Finally, adhere several appliqué flowers onto the body of the can using a hot-glue gun.

Create an entire set to organize your paper clips, rubber bands, cotton balls, and more!

MAKE & CREATE HAND TOWELS
FROM PAGE 65

Delight yourself and your guests with embellished hand towels!

SUPPLIES: measuring tape ✳ white hand towels ✳ trims ✳ pins ✳ ribbon ✳ scissors ✳ needle and thread or sewing machine

- With a measuring tape determine the width of each towel to determine the length of trim needed. Allow at least $\frac{1}{2}$" on each side to create a folded under, finished edge.

- Pin the trim in place about 2" above the bottom hem.

- Try layering several types of trim on the same towel for a more luxurious effect.

- Hand- or machine-stitch the trim or ribbon in place.

Experiment! Try decorating your favorite bath mat, kitchen towels, or an assortment of colored towels in this same way.

MAKE & CREATE CANDLES
FROM PAGE 71

Transform plain pillar candles into fanciful accessories for your home.

sᴜᴘᴘʟɪᴇs: an assortment of pillar candles (any shape, size, or color) ⁂ flexible plastic stencils ⁂ tape ⁂ paint (craft stores carry special paint for wax) ⁂ sponge or brush ⁂ hot-glue gun ⁂ embellishments

- Using a flexible plastic stencil, wrap and tape the stencil in the position where you desire the motif on the candle.

- Using paint on a sponge or paintbrush, fill in the stencil.

- Be fearless with layering of colors.

- Add some deliciousness to your candle by wrapping ribbon around the base.

- Try gluing costume jewelry, beads, buttons, or rhinestones to your creation.

Use a single pillar candle atop a decorative saucer to make a simple yet elegant statement . . . or display a collection of them atop your mantel, vanity, windowsill, or dining room table. Be creative!

MAKE & CREATE TASSELS
FROM PAGE 90

These tassels are especially easy to make—just dig through your treasures and use your imagination!

sᴜᴘᴘʟɪᴇs: a collection of new and old figurines ⁂ hot-glue gun ⁂ ribbon ⁂ trim ⁂ embellishments ⁂ scissors

- Turn small ceramic or resin figurines into beautiful ornaments by gluing ribbon, trims, tassels, and crystals to their bases with a hot-glue gun.

- Cut varying lengths of string and ribbon to hang your creations.

- If you don't have goodies like these at your fingertips, look for them at antique stores, garage sales, flea markets, or thrift shops.

These tassels also make great window shade pulls, decorative lamp chains, wall hangings, and more.

MAKE & CREATE SHELF
FROM PAGE 91

This charming Tracy Porter shelf can be found unfinished at select craft stores. Look for the Tracy Porter Make & Create™ statement at a craft retailer near you.

SUPPLIES: fine sandpaper ✳ latex paint ✳ stencils ✳ clear water-based polyurethane ✳ hot-glue gun ✳ striped and sheer ribbon ✳ silk flowers and leaves ✳ craft pearls ✳ embellishments

- Lightly sand the shelf.

- Paint the shelf one solid color—or be adventurous and paint the top, sides, and back one color, with the scalloped area and underneath a contrasting color. Let dry, sand lightly, and apply a second coat.

- Try decorating the top and sides using a stencil pattern and paint to give them the feel of vintage wallpaper.

- Apply an even coat of clear, water-based polyurethane.

- Using a hot-glue gun, glue striped ribbon on the front base of the shelf as shown.

- Glue sheer ribbon onto the front edge of the side brackets.

- Add flowers, leaves, pearls, or other embellishments to the scalloped area as a beautiful finishing touch.

TRACY PORTER MAKE & CREATE GUIDE

projects taken from Adding Layers

of Personality (pages 93–142)

Allow yourself the freedoom

to change your mind.

MAKE & CREATE EMBELLISHED DOORS
FROM PAGE 100

SUPPLIES: decorative wood or resin ornaments (available at most local craft stores) ✳ wood glue ✳ damp sponge or cloth ✳ masking tape ✳ latex paint ✳ brushes

- Select the desired motif for your door panels.

- Alternate the reliefs, or use identical ones for each panel for a more uniform look.

- Adhere the decorative ornaments using wood glue. Wipe away any excess glue with a damp sponge or cloth.

- Of course doors can be embellished while still on their hinges. You may want to tape the relief down after gluing to avoid slippage. Another option is to take the door off its hinges to work on a flat surface.

- When the glue has dried, paint the entire door in a solid color for a timeless, classic look.

If you want a more dramatic statement, try painting the relief a contrasting color before attaching it to the door.

MAKE & CREATE DECORATED DOORKNOBS
FROM PAGE 101

SUPPLIES: rhinestones ✳ doorknobs ✳ hot-glue gun ✳ millinery flowers ✳ pressed-glass flower

- Glue rhinestones around the outer edge of the doorknob using a hot-glue gun.

- Decide on a beautiful focal point for the knob. Here we've chosen a pink millinery flower, which we also attached using hot glue. A delicate pressed-glass flower is glued in the center of the knob as a simple yet elegant finishing touch.

If you don't have a vintage doorknob, try antiquing an ordinary one before embellishing. Simply basecoat the knob with a rich color; when dry, top with a high-gloss black paint and crackling glaze technique.

MAKE & CREATE EMBELLISHED
FIREPLACE MANTELS

FROM PAGES 136–137

SUPPLIES: decorative tile or plaque * pencil * putty knife * tile adhesive * embellishments * hot-glue gun

- Choose a decorative tile or plaque that inspires you. Here we've chosen a vintage ceramic plaque that we found at an antique store.

- Center the plaque on the front of your mantel. Use a pencil to mark its placement.

- Depending on the weight and material of your plaque, you can use a variety of adhesives to hold it firmly in place. For this particular project, we used a putty knife to spread a generous amount of tile adhesive evenly over the mantel surface to be covered by the plaque. Firmly press the plaque into the adhesive using a slight twisting motion. Allow the adhesive to dry thoroughly.

- Once in place, arrange your other embellishments and attach them using a hot-glue gun. Here we've used seashells, old jewelry and pearls, ceramic roses, and ribbon trim. Dream delicious!

MAKE & CREATE INSPIRATION BOX
FROM PAGE 139

This charming inspiration box can be found unfinished at select craft stores. Look for the Tracy Porter Make & Create™ statement at a craft retailer near you.

SUPPLIES: fine sandpaper ✳ paint ✳ brushes ✳ decorative stencils or rubber stamps ✳ decoupage medium ✳ clear water-based polyurethane ✳ craft or fabric glue ✳ decorative ribbon trim ✳ embellishments ✳ hot-glue gun

- Lightly sand the box before beginning.

- Basecoat the entire box in a solid color. Here we've chosen a soft yellow. Sand lightly. Let dry and apply a second coat.

- To mimic the look of fabric or wallpaper, use a plastic stencil or rubber stamp to create a patterned motif over the entire surface.

- We decoupaged a lovely butterfly on the front of this little box. You could achieve the same look through stencils, stickers, or hand painting.

- Protect your inspiration box with a clear coat of water-based polyurethane before adding other embellishments.

- Using craft or fabric glue, attach a decorative ribbon trim around the edge of the box lid.

- Add beads and rhinestones using a hot-glue gun.

TRACY PORTER MAKE & CREATE GUIDE

projects taken from Illuminating

Ideas (pages 143–184)

Drink in the beauty

that surrounds you.

MAKE & CREATE CRYSTALS
FROM PAGES 150–151

Inexpensive crystals can be found in most local craft stores, as well as craft-related mail-order catalogs or websites. Hang them as is, or embellish them as we've done here.

SUPPLIES: embellishments ✳ hot-glue gun ✳ scissors ✳ trim or fabric strips

- Use any baubles, new or old, to add a layer of whimsy to your crystals. Here we've used everything from beads, millinery flowers, old jewelry, ribbon, fabric remnants, feathers, rhinestones, and more.

- Glue embellishments in place using small amounts of hot glue.

- Cut and knot trim, ribbon, or fabric strips securely in place for hanging.

- These crystals have simply been colored using a watercolor art marker on the backside of the crystal. This gives them the appearance of stained or European glass.

TIP *hanging crystals*

We hung our assortment of fanciful window crystals using wire. You could also use scraps of ribbon, twine, yarn, string, even fishing line, depending on the look you are after. Simply cut to the length you want and hang where desired using nails or decorative hooks.

MAKE & CREATE CANDLEHOLDER
FROM PAGE 170

This charming Tracy Porter candleholder can be found unfinished at select craft stores. Look for the Tracy Porter Make & Create™ statement at a craft retailer near you.

SUPPLIES: fine sandpaper ❋ latex paint ❋ brushes ❋ stencils ❋ water-based clear polyurethane ❋ hot-glue gun ❋ embellishments

- Lightly sand the candleholder.

- Basecoat the top and sides of the candleholder in a solid color, or paint them two coordinating shades, as we've done. Let dry, sand lightly, and apply a second coat.

- Stencil on a decorative motif (such as flowers, leaves, insects, or scrolls) or paint the design free-hand. Use your imagination!

- Protect with a single coat of clear water-based polyurethane.

- Glue on your favorite accents—silk flowers, leaves, ribbon, or trim—whatever tickles your fancy!

Why not embellish a picture frame in the same way to set beside your new candleholder?

MAKE & CREATE LAMPSHADES
FROM PAGE 174

Dress up your old lampshades with some quick and simple embellishing techniques.

SUPPLIES: embellishments ✳ hot-glue gun ✳ scissors ✳ spray adhesive

A

B

C

D

A This plain linen shade was transformed with a simple row of vintage buttons, which were glued around the bottom rim using a hot-glue gun. Don't be afraid to layer your buttons for visual effect, as we've done. Choose tone-on-tone buttons for a classic look, or use a colorful assortment for a more striking statement.

B We wanted to accentuate the warm glow of this shade, so we added rich trims around the top and the bottom. Simply hold the trim around the shade and cut to the proper length, leaving about a 1-inch overlap in the back for gluing in place. To add interest, we used this beautiful vintage brooch atop the velvety grosgrain ribbon, held in place using a dab of hot glue.

C For nontextural or smooth shades, fabric and wallpaper remnants are an excellent way to add character. Cut the fabric or paper to the desired size and glue in place using spray adhesive. Add layers of millinery flowers, beads, rhinestones, and more. Fringes and tassels make lovely finishing embellishments for any lampshade. Simply cut to length and glue around the base of the shade.

D This wonderful antique lampshade needed just a touch of whimsy. By gluing vintage lace, silk ribbon, and a romantic grouping of millinery flowers around the bottom, we've made this shade fit for a princess!

Try painting or embellishing your lamp base to complement your new shade.

MAKE & CREATE SWITCH PLATES
FROM PAGE 175

Create beautiful switch plates out of ordinary plastic or wooden ones. Match them to your décor, or use your imagination to create fun and interesting conversation pieces.

SUPPLIES: latex or enamel paint ✳ stickers ✳ hot-glue gun or spray adhesive ✳ buttons ✳ embellishments ✳ ribbon ✳ brass tacks ✳ fabric or wallpaper remnants

- Remove old switch plates from the wall before beginning.

- If desired, basecoat the switch plate in your favorite color.

- Add charming stickers—here we've created switch plates for a children's room. To change the look entirely, you could use flowers, butterflies, and insects for a garden theme. What a great project for kids!

- Glue on vintage buttons, small brooches, beads, or colorful stones for a unique twist. You could even use an old necklace to frame the outside edges if you like.

- On a wooden switch plate, try gluing a ribbon border and securing the corners with brass tacks.

- Fabric and wallpaper can be a wonderful way to help your switch plate blend into the wall, or stand out as a decorative element.

Don't forget you will have to reattach your switch plates to the wall. You can add finishing embellishments, such as beads, buttons, silk flowers, or stickers, over the screws once they are in place on your wall.

TRACY PORTER COLOR GUIDE

Finding the "right" color can be one of the most gratifying yet challenging decorating dilemmas. We've extracted colors from some of our design studio archives that we hope will inspire you. Whether you are searching for a new wall color, upholstery, textiles, or even decorative accessories, we encourage you to utilize this color guide as a starting point.

With a compelling array of exciting colors, from neutral tones to richly saturated hues, we hope to offer you limitless options for your own decorating combinations. As long as the mix of colors is working for you . . . there is truly no wrong way to approach color. Consider pairing some of these stronger colors with neutrals for a classic look. Alternatively, you may want to try using several colors together for a dramatic feel. We encourage you to experiment with these palettes in ways that reflect your personality Jump in, trust yourself, and try some on!

DRAWN FROM NATURE

A HINT OF COLOR

A VIVID SPLASH

RICHLY SATURATED

TRACY PORTER RESOURCE GUIDE

OTHER HELPFUL RESOURCES

RESOURCE	TELEPHONE	WEBSITE
A B C Carpet & Home Company, Inc. • New York City flagship store • European chandeliers, unique accessories, furniture and antiques • Wide assortment of rugs and fabrics	212.473.3000	www.abchome.com
Ann Sacks Tile & Stone, Inc. • Resource catalog and showrooms nationwide • Wide assortment of unique ceramic and glass tile and stone	800.278.8453	www.annsacks.com
Anthropologie • Mail-order catalog and nationwide retail stores • Lifestyle retailer—trendy accessories and home furnishings	800.309.2500	www.anthropologie.com
Ballard Designs • Mail-order catalog • Great assortment of home accessories and furnishings—nicely priced	800.367.2775	www.ballarddesigns.com/home.jsp

RESOURCE	TELEPHONE	WEBSITE
Exposures • Mail-order catalog • Picture frames, photo boxes, photo albums, archival supplies	800.222.4947	www.exposuresonline.com
Hold Everything • Mail-order catalog • Baskets, wide variety of storage containers, closet organizers, home office accessories.	800.840.3596	www.williams-sonomainc.com/com/hld
IKEA • Mail-order catalog and nationwide retail stores • Inexpensive stylish basics for the home	800.434.4532	www.ikea.com
Kenneth Lynch and Sons • Very large assortment of reproduction stone garden ornaments and statuary, figures, finials, animals, fountains, sundials	203.762.8363	www.klynchandsons.com
M & J Trimming Company • New York City retail store • Ribbon, trimmings, charms, buttons, beads	212.842.5000	www.mjtrim.com
Pearl River Mart, Inc. • New York City retail store • Unique, very inexpensive Asian store • Feels very dime-store—fun for cheap tchotchkes	212.431.4770	no website
Tender Buttons • New York City retail store • Unique and enormous range of buttons for embellishing—enamel, glass, ceramic, porcelain	212.758.7004	no website

Tinsel Trading Company   212.730.1030   no website
- New York City retail store
- Trims, tassels, embellishments, vintage specialty trims

Tracy Porter   888.382.4500   www.tracyporter.com
- Princeton, Wisconsin, retail store
- Lifestyle store with comprehensive collection of products designed by Tracy Porter—rugs, pillows, dinnerware, glassware, books, stationery, framed art, furniture, candles, etc.—an inviting fantasy environment with many treasures

tracyporter.com   www.tracyporter.com/findastore.shtml
- Listings for stores across the country that carry home furnishings and lifestyle products designed by Tracy Porter

University Products—
The Archival Company   800.628.1912   www.archivalsuppliers.com
- Mail-order catalog
- Fabric, hat, book, and photo storage, photo conservation supplies

Van Dyke's Restorers   800.558.1234   www.vandykes.com
- Mail-order catalog
- Restoration supply company. Wide variety of reproduction hardware, embossed reliefs, decorative upholstery tacks, wood finials, textured or embossed wall coverings.